The *Master* Connector

The Ultimate Guide to Building Impactful Connections for Life & Business Success

WRITTEN BY
NICHOLE HARMON-POINTDUJOUR

Copyright © 2025 by Nichole Harmon-Pointdujour.

All rights reserved under the international and Pan-American copyright conventions.

Published by 1BrickPublishing. First published in the United States of America.

Printed in the United States.

ISBN: 978-1949303780 (Print) | ISBN: 978-1949303797 (Hardcover)

ISBN: 978-1949303834 (eBook)

All rights reserved. With the exception of brief quotations in a review, no part of this book may be reproduced or transmitted, in any form, or by any means, electronic or mechanical (including photocopying), nor may it be stored in any information storage and retrieval system without written permission from the publisher.

The advice contained in this material might not be suitable for everyone. The author designed the information to present her opinion about the subject matter. The reader must carefully investigate all aspects of any business decision before committing to himself or herself. The author obtained the information contained herein from sources she believes to be reliable and from her own personal experience, but she neither implies nor intends any guarantee of accuracy. The author is not in the business of giving legal, accounting, or any other type of professional advice. Should the reader need such advice, he or she must seek services from a competent professional. The author particularly disclaims any liability, loss, or risk taken by individuals who directly or indirectly act on the information contained herein. The author believes the advice presented here is sound, but readers cannot hold her responsible for either the actions they take or the risks taken by individuals who directly or indirectly act on the information contained herein.

Author Photo by - Tangie Renee Photography
Hair by - Keaona Curington

Make up - Marlissa Cunningham - Timmons

Dedication

To my grandparents, who paved the way with their resilience, and to my parents Valerie Harmon-Parker and Brian Parker, who instilled in me the belief that I could achieve anything. Your sacrifices built the foundation for my success, and I am forever grateful.

To my family, friends, and mentors—your love, guidance, and unwavering support have shaped me into the woman I am today.

To my husband, my rock, and my greatest supporter—your love, encouragement, and belief in me push me to be my best every day. Thank you for always standing by my side and uplifting me in every season of life.

To every dreamer from the inner city striving for more—may this book be a reminder that your network, your reputation, and your willingness to step into new circles can transform your life.

And above all, to God—who gave me the vision for *The Master Connector Agency* and continues to guide my path. Without You, none of this would be possible.

A Call to Share the Keys to Successful Networking

Please share this book with anyone whom you feel would benefit from its guidance, inspiration, and actionable steps for building powerful relationships, leveraging connections for career and business success, and mastering the art of networking to create life-changing opportunities.

Contents

Foreword by Angela Yee 1

Introduction: The Power of Authentic Connection 5

Chapter 1: From Inner City to Inner Circles 15

Chapter 2: The First Rule of Networking: Leading with Value 29

Chapter 3: The Art of the Follow-Through 47

Chapter 4: Breaking Bread, Breaking Barriers 61

Chapter 5: Bridging Different Worlds 77

Chapter 6: Investing in Access: Strategic Positioning 91

Chapter 7: Business Resource Groups as Connection Accelerators 119

Chapter 8: Building Your Personal Brand Through Relationships 143

Chapter 9: Converting Connections to Opportunities . . 169

Chapter 10: Digital Age Networking 203

Chapter 11: Faith, Purpose, and Connection 235

Chapter 12: The Ripple Effect: Creating a Connection

Legacy	261
Final Thoughts: Your Connection Journey Begins	289
Acknowledgements	299
About the Author	301
Praise for The Master Connector	305

Foreword

by Angela Yee

"Hey Angela, are you at Black Entrepreneurs Day? Joy, who I wanted to introduce you to about the business mentorship, is there too. Let me know if you want me to connect you two."

This is one of the text messages I received from Nichole. I previously mentioned to her that I was having challenges in managing and scaling my business, and her mind went to work with her mental rolodex of who she could refer to help me. Nichole already had my full trust because of our prior interactions, many of which I wasn't even present for. Word traveled back to me that she brought my name up in rooms I wasn't in and pushed for me to be considered for opportunities at Fortune 500 companies. Do you know how valuable it is to have a person advocating for you behind closed doors, with no ulterior motives?

I learned the impact of connections early in my career, but it wasn't something I considered a business until almost a decade later. There were times when I would "hook people up" with each other and proudly know I helped make a deal come to fruition, only to never get an acknowledgment or even a thank you, much less a fee. It wasn't until I facilitated a meeting between Reebok and TDE, when Top Dawg showed up to sign the deal, that I actually got a check for it. I was told that he walked into the meeting and said, "Make sure y'all break Angela off because I wouldn't be here if she didn't make it happen." And they did. It was a demand I never even considered.

Nichole has a reputation for connecting the dots. That's why she earned the moniker "the master connector. "We ended up having a conversation about why she needed to turn this into a business, where her agency links people together who complement each other's needs. It is mind-boggling how many corporations don't have the cultural competence to curate a panel, much less a campaign, that is relevant to the community. That's where Nichole's superpowers excel.

The problem was that even with her MBA and her extensive travels (44 countries and counting), volunteer work, and financial and business leadership, she still viewed being a master connector as passion work and favors.

"Nichole, you have literally made people millions of dollars. This is your business. People who deserve it but would have never been considered. You have forged authentic relationships and mentorships for others, and yes, it feels good, but it's a business."

The popular catchphrase "your net worth is your network" rings true and always will. According to recent data, referrals are four times more likely to be hired than other candidates and to retain their positions. Sponsorships in the workplace have proven to be valuable because you have an established person advocating for you and putting their reputation on the line.

I wouldn't be where I am today, as a Radio Hall of Fame recipient, entrepreneur, and host of my own nationally syndicated show "Way Up with Angela Yee" on iHeartRadio, without the connections I made in the music industry and beyond. I am still growing my network, and having the support of someone like Nichole is invaluable. She is a proven and trusted source who can send out a text, email, or mention my name in conversations in a positive manner, which leads to another level. This book will give you strategies, insights, and the confidence to go way up!

Angela Yee,
Hall of Fame Radio Personality
Real Estate Investor
Host of the Nationally Syndicated Show "Way Up with Angela Yee"

INTRODUCTION

The Power of Authentic Connection

The dining room buzzed with energy, as Atlanta's top leaders gathered for my quarterly Master Connector dinner—one of the city's most coveted invitations. Corporate executives exchanged ideas with entertainment moguls, tech entrepreneurs connected with the Mayor and other civic leaders, and conversations flowed as effortlessly as the wine. As I watched these powerful individuals connect, share ideas, and plant the seeds for future collaborations, I couldn't help but smile. This was exactly what I had envisioned when God gave me the inspiration to create these gatherings—a space where artificial barriers dissolved and genuine relationships could flourish.

Yet, just twenty years earlier, I never could have imagined hosting events like this. Growing up in the inner cities of New Jersey, my world was small, and my understanding of "networking" was limited to the tight-knit community around me. Back then, I was more focused on finding creative ways to cut class than on building professional connections. The path that led me from those humble beginnings to becoming an equity trader on Wall Street and eventually founding The Master Connector Agency was paved with relationships—countless moments of genuine connection that opened doors I didn't even know existed.

That's the funny thing about authentic connection: it has a way of expanding your horizons beyond what you thought possible. Every major milestone in my journey, from being the first in my family to attend college to landing coveted positions in investment banking and Equity Trading, came through relationships with people who saw potential in me and were willing to extend a hand. But here's what I learned along the way: those relationships weren't about collecting business cards or strategic networking. They were about genuine human connection, about leading with how I could help others rather than what I could gain.

This book is your guide to mastering the art of authentic connection—the kind that transforms lives and creates lasting impact. Whether you're an entrepreneur looking to scale your business, a professional aiming to climb the corporate ladder, or simply someone who wants to expand their circle of influence, the principles I share here will help you build the kinds of relationships that open doors and create opportunities.

Why Connection Matters Now More Than Ever

We live in an age of unprecedented connectivity—the most connected era in history. A few taps on our phones can put us in touch with almost anyone, and our social media networks stretch into the thousands. Yet, paradoxically, many of us feel more disconnected than ever. We have countless LinkedIn contacts, but few real mentors. We collect Instagram followers, but struggle to find true collaborators. We're connected, but not connecting.

This disconnect carries real consequences in both our personal and professional lives. In today's complex business landscape, success rarely comes through solo effort. The most significant opportunities—whether that's landing a dream job, securing investment for your startup, or making that game-changing deal—almost always come through relationships. But not just any relationships. They come through authentic connections built on trust, mutual value, and genuine care for others' success.

I've witnessed this truth play out countless times throughout my career. When I was a fresh graduate from Virginia Union University (an HBCU that most of my Wall Street colleagues had never heard of), it wasn't my resume alone that landed me a coveted position at one of the world's top investment banks. It was a connection with a former classmate who believed in my potential and was willing to recommend me. When I later moved to Atlanta and launched my own business, it wasn't fancy marketing strategies that filled my first event with 150 of the city's most influential leaders.

It was the strength of the relationships I'd cultivated over years of genuinely serving others and adding value wherever I could.

The Missing Piece in Most Networking Advice

If you've read other books about networking or building professional relationships, you've probably encountered plenty of tactical advice: how to work a room, perfect your elevator pitch, or optimize your LinkedIn profile. While these skills have their place, they miss the most crucial element of powerful connection—authenticity.

True connection isn't about techniques or tactics. It's about approaching relationships with genuine curiosity, empathy, and a desire to serve. It's about seeing the human being behind the title and understanding that everyone—from the CEO to the security guard—has value to offer and stories to share. This human-first approach to relationship building has been my secret weapon throughout my career, allowing me to build bridges between corporate boardrooms and creative communities, between established institutions and emerging innovators.

Take, for example, my experience with one of the world's top motivational speakers. When I first met him at an event, I didn't approach him with an agenda or ask for anything. Instead, I listened to him share about his vision for building generational wealth for his family. I offered to connect him with a business mentorship program. For years, I supported his initiatives, attended his events, and helped book speakers for his conferences—all without asking for anything in return. When I finally did reach out for support with my own ventures years later, the response was immediate and enthusiastic. That's the power of authentic connection and playing the long game in relationships.

Breaking Down Barriers Through Connection

One of the most powerful aspects of authentic connection is its ability to break down barriers—whether they're cultural, social, or professional. Throughout my career, I've often found myself in spaces where I was the only Black woman, the only person from an HBCU, or the only one who grew up in the inner city. These experiences taught me valuable lessons about bridging different worlds and creating understanding across divides.

I remember sitting on the trading floor early in my career, hearing colleagues discuss their parents giving them $60,000 for weddings and house down payments—amounts that would have been unimaginable in my community. Rather than letting these differences create distance, I learned to use them as opportunities for connection and understanding. I shared my own experiences openly while remaining curious about others' perspectives. This ability to move authentically between different worlds has become one of my greatest strengths, allowing me to create unique value by bringing diverse groups together.

Today, through The Master Connector Agency, I purposefully create spaces where these barriers can dissolve. At our events, you'll find corporate executives breaking bread with creative entrepreneurs, established leaders mentoring rising stars, and meaningful connections forming across traditional industry lines. These interactions often lead to surprising collaborations and opportunities that benefit everyone involved.

The Master Connector Method

Throughout this book, I'll share the specific principles and practices that have helped me build powerful connections throughout my career. But before we dive into the tactical elements, it's important to understand the core philosophy that underlies everything I teach.

The Master Connector Method is built on six key principles:

1. **Lead with Value:** Always start by asking how you can help others. This simple shift sets you apart from 90% of people who lead with what they want.
2. **Do Good Business:** Your reputation is everything. Whatever you commit to, deliver it with excellence. Under-promise and over-deliver. This builds trust and makes people eager to recommend and work with you.
3. **Follow Through:** Connections fade without follow-up. The fortune is in the follow-up.

INTRODUCTION: THE POWER OF AUTHENTIC CONNECTION

4. **Invest in Access:** Sometimes you need to be willing to invest in putting yourself in the right rooms. Whether that's buying a first-class ticket, joining a particular organization, or attending certain events, strategic investments in access can pay massive dividends.
5. **Build Genuine Relationships:** See people beyond their titles. Take time to understand their goals, struggles, and dreams.
6. **Play the Long Game:** The most valuable connections often take years to bear fruit. Be patient and focus on building genuine relationships rather than seeking immediate returns.

These principles have helped me build a network that spans from Wall Street boardrooms to entertainment industry gatherings, from corporate C-suites to community organizations. More importantly, they've helped me create a genuine impact by connecting people and opportunities in ways that create value for everyone involved.

What You'll Learn in This Book

In the chapters that follow, I'll take you on a journey through my experiences, while equipping you with practical strategies for building your own powerful network. We'll explore:

1. How my journey from the inner city to inner circles taught me foundational lessons in authentic connection

2. Why leading with value is the first rule of effective networking
3. The art of follow-through and how to maintain relationships over time
4. How breaking bread together creates unique opportunities for meaningful connection
5. Strategies for bridging different worlds and cultures through authentic engagement
6. The power of strategic positioning and investing in access
7. How to leverage business resource groups for connection acceleration
8. Building your personal brand through relationships rather than self-promotion
9. Converting connections into opportunities without being transactional
10. Navigating digital networking while maintaining authenticity
11. Aligning your connections with deeper purpose and faith
12. Creating a ripple effect that extends your impact far beyond direct relationships

Each chapter includes practical exercises, real-world examples, and specific action steps you can take to implement these principles in your own life and career. You'll also find **"Connection Gems"** - key insights and takeaways that you can apply immediately.

Who This Book Is For

While the principles in this book can benefit anyone looking to build better relationships, I've written it specifically for:

- Professionals looking to advance their careers through strategic relationships
- Entrepreneurs seeking to build valuable connections for their businesses
- Students aiming to build future success through relationships and strategic connections
- Community leaders wanting to create meaningful impact through collaboration
- Anyone feeling stuck in their current network and wanting to expand their circle of influence
- Those who want to become master connectors in their own right

Whether you're just starting your professional journey or you're already established in your field, you'll find valuable insights and practical strategies you can apply immediately.

A Personal Invitation

As you read this book, I invite you to approach it with an open mind and heart. The strategies I share aren't just theoretical - they're battle-tested through years of experience in both corporate and entrepreneurial settings. They've helped me navigate from the inner city to Wall Street, from employee to entrepreneur, and from outsider to trusted connector.

More importantly, I invite you to remember that at its core, connection is about people. It's about seeing the humanity in others and allowing them to see yours. It's about creating value and making a positive impact in others' lives. When you approach relationship building from this perspective, the possibilities are endless.

So, let's begin this journey together. Whether your goal is to advance your career, grow your business, or simply build more meaningful relationships, the principles in this book will help you become a master connector in your own right. Welcome to the art and science of authentic connection.

Remember, your network is your net worth - but only when those connections are built on a foundation of genuine relationship and mutual value. Let's learn how to create exactly that.

CHAPTER 1

From Inner City to Inner Circles

"Your circumstances don't determine your destination - your connections do."

The buzzing fluorescent lights of Virginia Union University's business school illuminated the plaque on the wall - the Dean's List. I stood there, mesmerized by my friend Keisha's name proudly displayed among the top students. "How did you get your name up there?" I asked, genuinely curious. Her answer was simple: "You just need to get A's and B's." That moment changed everything for me. Not just because it motivated me to improve my grades, but because it taught me one of the most valuable lessons about connection: sometimes the most important relationships aren't with powerful executives or industry leaders - they're with the peers right beside you who can open your eyes to possibilities you never knew existed.

But let me back up. To understand how I became The Master Connector, you need to understand where my journey began. Because the truth is, every principle I teach about building powerful connections was shaped by my experiences growing up in the inner cities of New Jersey, where I learned my first lessons about the power of authentic relationships.

Early Lessons in Connection

I was born in Newark, New Jersey, to a teenage mother who herself was born to teenage parents. My grandmother had my mother at sixteen, and my mother had me at nineteen. This cycle of teenage pregnancy was common in our community, a pattern that seemed destined to repeat itself generation after generation. But patterns are meant to be broken—and it's often connections that help us break them.

My early years were spent moving between various inner-city neighborhoods—Newark, Irvington, East Orange, and finally Vauxhall. These communities, while often labeled as "disadvantaged" by outsiders, taught me invaluable lessons about human connection. In the inner city, relationships weren't just nice to have—they were essential for survival and growth.

> **CONNECTION GEM:** *Your first network is your community. Never underestimate the power of grassroots connections and the lessons they can teach you about authentic relationship building.*

My mother, despite her young age, understood the importance of expanding my horizons beyond our immediate environment. Through a connection she had built, she managed to get my brother and me into a Jewish summer camp—an experience that would become my first lesson in bridging different worlds.

This camp was my first exposure to how differently other people lived. While my campmates were planning trips to Israel and around the world, my mother could only afford to send me on day trips to Hershey Park. But rather than letting these differences create distance, I learned to use them as opportunities for connection and understanding. I observed how these families operated, how they communicated, and how they built and maintained relationships. Without realizing it, I was developing the cultural intelligence that would later help me navigate corporate boardrooms and professional environments.

The Power of Maternal Connection

My mother's influence on my journey cannot be overstated. Despite not having a college degree herself, she had an instinctive understanding of the power of connections and opportunities. When we moved from Essex County to Union County, she maintained a relationship with Mr. Ponder, the director of Upward Bound, a college prep program. This program was technically only for Essex County residents, but through my mother's connection and advocacy, my brother and I were allowed to continue participating.

> **CONNECTION GEM:** *Sometimes the most powerful connections come through advocates who believe in your potential. Be willing to both seek and become such an advocate.*

This was a crucial lesson in the power of maintaining relationships even when immediate benefits aren't apparent. My mother couldn't have known when she first met Mr. Ponder how important that connection would become, but she nurtured it anyway. This principle—maintaining relationships without expecting immediate returns—would later become a cornerstone of my networking philosophy.

Breaking Patterns Through Connection

My high school years weren't exactly a model of academic excellence. I was smart enough to pass tests but spent more time figuring out how to cut class than actually attending it. I'd come home with C's and B's, proud of managing decent grades, despite minimal attendance. My father, however, refused to congratulate this underachievement. "If you would just show up to class," he'd say, "you'd get straight A's."

This tough love was paired with unwavering support. Every morning at 6 AM, my father would wake up to run with me as I trained for varsity track. This daily ritual taught me another crucial lesson about connection: consistency builds trust. My father didn't just tell me to take my training seriously—he showed up every day, demonstrating through actions rather than words that he was invested in my success.

> **CONNECTION GEM:** *The strongest connections are built through consistent actions, not just words. Show up reliably for others, and they'll show up for you.*

But perhaps the most significant pattern-breaking connection came through my mother's involvement with Upward Bound. This program exposed me to something no one in my family had achieved: a college education. Through Upward Bound, I went on college tours, learned about higher education opportunities, and most importantly, saw that another path was possible.

The College Connection

When I arrived at Virginia Union University, I was the first person in my family to attend college. I had no roadmap, no family experience to draw from, and no understanding of academic terms like "Dean's List" or "internship." But what I did have was an ability to build relationships—a skill that would prove more valuable than any academic preparation.

That moment standing in front of the Dean's List plaque with Keisha was pivotal. After learning what it took to get on that list, I completely changed my approach to education. I started sitting in the front of classes, engaging with professors, and taking my studies seriously. By my final semester, I had achieved a 3.8 GPA.

But the real power of this connection wasn't just about academic motivation. Keisha's influence created a domino effect of opportunities. Because I was now on the Dean's List, I caught the attention of the Career Services leader, who introduced me to the concept of internships. This led to my first corporate experience at Nationwide in their HR department—a far cry from my retail job at Old Navy, where I had been proudly anticipating a raise to $7.83 per hour.

> **CONNECTION GEM:** *One strong connection can create a cascade of opportunities. Focus on building genuine relationships rather than just chasing specific outcomes.*

The Cultural Shift

My college years also taught me valuable lessons about navigating different economic realities—lessons that would prove crucial in my later career. It was during this time that I first realized I had grown up with limited financial resources. This awareness came when my college friend easily called her father for $300 to buy textbooks, while I had to figure out creative solutions when my mother couldn't provide the same.

These experiences taught me how to bridge worlds without losing authenticity. I learned to understand and operate in environments that were very different from my upbringing while staying true to who I was. This skill would become invaluable as I built connections across various social and professional spheres.

The Power of Peer Connection

The most life-changing connection of my college years came through a classmate named Franklin. He had secured an opportunity to work in the technology department at one of the top financial institutions in the world. Because we had built a genuine relationship through our shared classes, he thought of me when he learned about opportunities in operations and investment banking.

This connection led to a series of interviews that would ultimately change my life. The program typically only recruited from Ivy League schools and required a 3.75 GPA with an MBA. I had the grades but came from an HBCU that many of my interviewers had never heard of. Yet Franklin's recommendation got me in the door, and my ability to connect authentically during the interviews did the rest.

> **CONNECTION GEM:** *Never underestimate the power of peer relationships. Your classmates and colleagues today could be the ones opening doors for you tomorrow.*

Wall Street Lessons in Connection

Landing on Wall Street as a young Black woman from the inner city who attended an HBCU was like stepping into another world. The culture shock was significant—from the way people dressed to how they communicated to their financial realities. I remember a colleague casually mentioning how her parents were giving her $30,000 for her wedding and $30,000 for a house down payment. This was more money than anyone in my family had ever had at once.

Rather than letting these differences intimidate me, I used them as opportunities to learn and grow. I joined business resource groups (BRGs) not just for Black employees or women, but also for veterans, LGBTQ+ employees, and other groups I wasn't personally part of. This taught me the importance of building connections across different communities and understanding various perspectives.

> **CONNECTION GEM:** *True connection comes from a willingness to step outside your comfort zone and understand perspectives different from your own.*

The Investment Banking Challenge

The investment banking program was incredibly demanding. I had to pass Excel tests, market tests, PowerPoint tests, and complete a 24-page case study within 24 hours. The program accepted only 40 people out of 40,000 applications, and I was competing against graduates from Harvard, Yale, and Princeton.

But here's where my background became an advantage rather than a hindrance. Growing up in the inner city had taught me how to adapt quickly, how to read people and situations, and how to build authentic connections across differences. These skills helped me navigate the corporate environment and build relationships with colleagues from very different backgrounds.

> **CONNECTION GEM:** *Your unique background and experiences are assets in building connections. Don't try to hide them—learn to leverage them.*

Learning Corporate Navigation

Early in my career, I faced various challenges, including microaggressions and cultural differences. There was the time a manager pulled me aside to discuss my hair, suggesting that senior management had concerns about how I presented myself compared to my white counterparts. Rather than becoming defensive, I used this as an opportunity to educate and build understanding, explaining how my professional appearance and work performance were separate issues.

This experience taught me valuable lessons about maintaining authenticity while building bridges. I learned to address difficult conversations directly, but diplomatically, to stand firm in my identity while finding common ground with others, and to turn potential conflicts into opportunities for connection and understanding.

The Power of Administrative Connections

One of the most valuable lessons I learned on Wall Street was the importance of building relationships at all levels. While many focused on connecting with executives and managing directors, I made sure to build genuine relationships with administrative assistants, security guards, and support staff. These connections often proved more valuable than those with senior executives.

> **CONNECTION GEM:** *Treat everyone with the same level of respect and attention. The person you ignore today might be the gatekeeper to your next opportunity tomorrow.*

The Turning Point

My career took an unexpected turn when I decided to move to Atlanta for love. I left my position as an equity trader in New

York, moving to a city where I had no professional network. This transition taught me perhaps the most valuable lesson about connection: sometimes you have to let go of what you have to create space for something better.

When I first arrived in Atlanta, I applied for positions that were beneath my experience level, just trying to get my foot in the door. To my surprise, I was rejected. But three months later, the same company reached out with an opportunity that was far better than what I had initially applied for—a national role that aligned perfectly with my skills and passion for helping others.

> **CONNECTION GEM:** *Sometimes a 'no' is just a 'not yet.' Maintain positive relationships even when things don't go as planned.*

The Birth of The Master Connector

The idea for The Master Connector Agency came through divine inspiration. After years of people telling me I should start a business because of my connection-building abilities, I finally understood my true gift. It wasn't just about knowing people—it was about bringing them together in ways that created value for everyone involved. God gave me the vision; He said, "You're going to create a space where you bring together your powerful network from corporate executives to industry leaders, and you are going to call it 'the rooms where the deals are done.'"

I launched the agency with a clear vision: to create spaces where corporate executives, industry leaders, and entrepreneurs could come together to form authentic connections and create meaningful opportunities. Within 120 days of launching, we had hosted successful events, secured corporate sponsorship, and built a growing membership community.

> **CONNECTION GEM:** *Your greatest gift might be something you do so naturally that you don't even recognize it as special. Pay attention to what others consistently praise you for.*

Looking Back, Looking Forward

As I reflect on my journey from the inner cities of New Jersey to the boardrooms of Wall Street and now to leading The Master Connector Agency, I'm struck by how each step was facilitated by authentic connections. From my mother's relationship with Mr. Ponder that got me into Upward Bound, to Keisha showing me the Dean's List, to Franklin recommending me for a position at one of the world's top financial institutions—each connection built upon the last, creating a bridge to new opportunities.

This journey has taught me that authentic connection isn't about business cards or LinkedIn connections—it's about seeing people for who they truly are and allowing them to see you. Every relationship, no matter how small, has the power to change the trajectory of your life. The right connection, at the right moment, can unlock doors you never even knew existed.

> **CONNECTION GEM:** *Your journey is your message. Every experience, every challenge, and every triumph gives you unique insight into building authentic connections.*

Chapter Takeaways

1. Authentic connections can break generational patterns and open new possibilities.
2. Your background and challenges can become your greatest assets in building relationships.
3. Peer connections are often as valuable as connections with those in positions of power.
4. Treat everyone with equal respect and attention—you never know who might open the next door.
5. Sometimes the most valuable connections come through unexpected sources.
6. Your unique journey gives you special insight into building authentic relationships.
7. Divine inspiration and purpose can guide you to your true calling in connection building.

Action Steps

1. Reflect on your journey and identify key connections that have influenced your path.
2. List three people from your past with whom you should reconnect.
3. Identify areas where your background gives you unique insight or advantage.
4. Write down three ways you can add value to your existing connections.
5. Look for opportunities to bridge different worlds or communities in your network.

Remember, your journey to becoming a master connector starts with understanding your own story and the lessons it has taught you about authentic connection. In the next chapter, we'll explore specific strategies for building and maintaining powerful relationships that can transform your life and career.

CHAPTER 2

The First Rule of Networking: Leading with Value

"The most powerful question in networking isn't 'What can you do for me?' but 'How can I help you?'"

I got invited to participate in a panel in Atlanta, and one of the panelists who was on stage with me was the number one motivational speaker in the world. We had briefly met in NYC prior at a Forbes event where he was the keynote speaker. After the event, a long line of eager fans formed around him. I stood back and observed. Almost everyone asked for something: "Can you help me with…?" "Would you be willing to…?" With each request, I saw his shoulders tense ever so slightly. He smiled, nodding politely, but I could see it—his energy was depleting with every ask.

When I spoke to him in the green room, I took a different approach. "I love your vision for building generational wealth," I said. "I work with a program that helps entrepreneurs scale their businesses. I'd be happy to share some information about it if that would be valuable to you." His expression changed immediately; he visibly perked up, asked questions about the program, and our conversation flowed naturally from there.

This small moment illustrates what I consider the first and most fundamental rule of networking: always lead with value. In a world where most people approach relationships asking what they can get, leading with what you can give immediately sets you apart.

The Value-First Mindset

Years later, at a business conference in Chicago, I saw the same pattern play out. During the networking reception, attendees circled the room in a familiar dance—exchanging business cards, pitching their services, and trying to extract value rather than create it.

Rather than joining this transactional exchange, I decided to take a different approach. As I spoke with each person, I focused entirely on understanding their business challenges and goals. When speaking with Maria, the owner of a growing marketing agency, I learned she was struggling to find reliable freelance writers with specific industry expertise.

"I know someone who might be perfect for what you need," I told her. "She has ten years of experience in that industry and is looking to build her freelance portfolio. Would you like me to introduce you?"

Maria's relief was immediate. "That would be amazing," she said. "I've been searching for months."

I made the introduction the very next day, connecting Maria with Sophia, a talented writer in my network who had recently left the corporate world. The match was perfect; Maria got the expertise she needed, and Sophia gained a valuable client. Neither was in a position to directly advance my career or business interests, but that wasn't the point.

> **CONNECTION GEM:** *Leading with value isn't a networking tactic—it's a relationship philosophy. When you consistently approach interactions thinking about how you can add value, you naturally build stronger connections.*

This value-first mindset transforms how you approach every interaction. Instead of entering conversations thinking about what you might gain, you approach them thinking about what you might contribute. This shift isn't just more effective—it's more fulfilling. Networking becomes less about strategic transactions and more about genuine human connection and service.

The 90/10 Rule of Networking

During a workshop I conducted for young professionals in New Jersey, I asked participants to describe their typical approach to networking events. Overwhelmingly, they focused on what they hoped to get: job leads, client connections, mentor relationships, or investment opportunities. When I asked how many entered networking situations primarily thinking about what they could offer others, only three hands out of nearly fifty went up.

Over the years, I've noticed a clear pattern: 90% of people approach networking with a 'What can I get?' mindset. Only 10% lead with 'How can I add value?' That small percentage? They're the ones who build the most meaningful, lasting connections. This creates an extraordinary opportunity—by simply flipping this approach, you immediately stand out in almost any professional or social setting.

I've seen this principle play out repeatedly in my own career. When most people approached senior leaders at industry conferences with requests or pitches, I focused on finding ways to support their initiatives or solve problems they'd mentioned in their presentations. This didn't just lead to more meaningful conversations; it created authentic relationships that developed naturally over time.

CHAPTER 2: THE FIRST RULE OF NETWORKING: LEADING WITH VALUE

> **CONNECTION GEM:** *Being part of the 10% who lead with value doesn't just make you stand out—it makes your networking efforts exponentially more effective.*

The reason most people get networking wrong is simple: immediate needs focus their attention. When you're looking for a job, seeking clients, or trying to raise capital, those pressing needs can dominate your thinking. This creates a transactional approach where relationships are viewed primarily as means to an end rather than meaningful connections.

This short-term thinking often reflects a scarcity mindset—a fear that giving without the certainty of receiving could leave you at a disadvantage. Yet paradoxically, this self-protective approach yields fewer results than generous contribution.

I've found that shifting to a value-first approach requires trust—trust that generosity creates opportunities in unexpected ways, and that authentic contribution builds a network far more powerful than strategic calculation could ever achieve.

Beyond reciprocity, value-leading creates positive associations. People naturally enjoy spending time with those who make them feel good, who lift them up, who offer help without asking for anything in return. This positive feeling becomes associated with you, making others more inclined to maintain and deepen the relationship.

The contrast effect also works in your favor. When most networkers focus on taking, your giving approach stands out sharply. This distinctiveness makes you more memorable and creates a stronger impression.

Perhaps most importantly, leading with value builds trust. When you demonstrate through actions rather than words that you're genuinely interested in others' success, you establish yourself as someone who can be trusted. This foundation of trust is essential for any meaningful professional relationship. I always lead with how I can help you or what big projects you are working on this year, and I think of ways I can add value to help them.

Value Assessment: Understanding What Matters

When I meet people, I ask them what they are working on and what their goals are for the year. I listen intently to how I can potentially help them achieve their goals. I go through my mental Rolodex of who is in that field that can offer them support, advice, or overall mentorship. I always lead with how I can add value.

During a catch-up in New York, a high-profile friend confided in me: "I need more exposure in the corporate world." I listened, filed it away, and later reached out to my contacts in the conference space. A few weeks later, she was headlining a Fortune 500 event as a keynote speaker. No ask, no pitch—just value, delivered. Because she is high-profile, people are always asking her for stuff, so I was happy that I took the time to listen and understand her goals and was able to get her the exposure that she wanted in the corporate space.

> **CONNECTION GEM:** *The ability to accurately assess what someone values is as important as your ability to provide that value. Develop your "value intelligence" by practicing thoughtful observation and inquiry.*

This experience taught me that value assessment requires careful attention and genuine curiosity. Value isn't one-size-fits-all—it varies tremendously based on professional context, personal situation, career stage, cultural background, and personality type.

To assess value effectively, I've learned to ask open-ended questions that reveal what matters most to people at this moment in their lives. Questions like "What's your biggest challenge right now?" or "What are you most excited about in your work currently?" often reveal far more than direct inquiries about how you might help.

Active listening is equally important—paying attention not just to what people say but how they say it, what they emphasize, what lights them up, or causes concern. These subtle cues often reveal what they truly value.

Perhaps most importantly, I've learned to identify pain points—the frustrations, obstacles, or challenges that cause stress or difficulty.

Addressing these pain points often creates more immediate value than supporting already successful endeavors.

Types of Value You Can Offer

Too many people believe that leading with value requires money, influence, or an elite network. It doesn't. The most impactful forms of value cost nothing, but thoughtfulness and effort.

I learned this lesson early in my career when I was just starting out with few professional connections and limited resources. What I did have was time, enthusiasm, and a willingness to help. When attending industry events, I would volunteer to help organizers with registration, participant coordination, or social media coverage. This not only gave me legitimate reasons to interact with speakers and attendees, but also allowed me to contribute meaningfully despite my junior status.

During one such event, I noticed that a prominent leader was struggling with technical issues before her presentation. While others watched passively, I stepped in to help resolve the problem. That small act of assistance led to a conversation after her talk, which eventually developed into a valuable mentoring relationship. My value in that moment wasn't about industry influence or connections; it was simply being observant and willing to help solve an immediate problem.

CHAPTER 2: THE FIRST RULE OF NETWORKING: LEADING WITH VALUE

> **CONNECTION GEM:** *Everyone has value to offer, regardless of position or resources. Identify your unique forms of value and learn to share them effectively.*

Over the years, I've recognized that value comes in many forms beyond the obvious monetary or professional benefits:

- **Information** - sharing useful knowledge or insights
- **Connections** - introducing people to helpful contacts
- **Resources** - providing access to tools, materials, or platforms
- **Skills and expertise** - helping others overcome obstacles
- **Opportunity creation** - facilitating exposure or advancement
- **Different perspectives** - offering a unique viewpoint or feedback
- **Support** - providing encouragement or understanding
- **Time and attention** - genuinely listening and being present
- **Recognition** - acknowledging others' accomplishments
- **Simplification** - making complex things easier or more manageable

I always make sure I lead with a compliment. Everyone loves a compliment, and it costs you nothing to give one and make the other person feel good.

Real-World Value-Leading Strategies

Different contexts call for different approaches to leading with value. Over the years, I've developed strategies that work effectively in various professional settings.

At industry conferences, I prepare differently than most attendees. Instead of just planning my own agenda, I research speakers and attendees ahead of time, looking for potential connection points or needs I might address. This allows me to approach conversations with specific, relevant value to offer.

> **CONNECTION GEM:** *Make value-leading a habit, not just a networking strategy. Look for ways to help others in all aspects of your life.*

Even in everyday interactions, the value-leading approach creates meaningful connections. When a colleague mentions an interest in mindfulness practices, I might share a helpful article or app recommendation. When someone is celebrating a work anniversary on LinkedIn, a specific, thoughtful comment acknowledging their contributions stands out amid generic congratulations.

What makes these strategies effective is their emphasis on genuine helpfulness rather than strategic positioning. When you approach interactions with a true desire to contribute something useful, people respond to that authenticity. The focus shifts from "networking" as a professional obligation to human connection as a meaningful exchange.

Story: The Power of Patience in Value-Leading

My relationship with Eric Thomas, one of the world's top motivational speakers, demonstrates the power of value-leading over time. When we first met at an event, I didn't ask for anything. Instead, I learned about his goals and later connected him to a free business mentorship program.

For years, I supported his initiatives—attending his daughter's birthday parties, helping book speakers for his conferences, and actively participating in his community—all without asking for anything in return. When I finally did reach out for support with my own ventures nearly a decade later, his response was immediate and enthusiastic.

This experience taught me that patience matters tremendously in value-leading. Real relationship building isn't about quick exchanges but about consistent support over time. The strongest bonds develop through regular, sustained value rather than isolated gestures.

> **CONNECTION GEM:** *Value-leading is often about playing the long game. The most powerful connections come from consistent value provided over time without expectation of immediate return.*

This long-term approach contrasts sharply with transactional networking, where the expectation of immediate reciprocity often creates pressure rather than genuine connection. When you provide value consistently without keeping score, you build a foundation of trust and goodwill that far exceeds what any strategic networking could achieve.

The relationship also taught me that authenticity resonates far more powerfully than calculation. Eric could easily distinguish between those who supported him strategically for what they might gain and those, like me, who genuinely believed in his mission and wanted to contribute to his success.

Perhaps most importantly, I learned that value compounds over time. Each small contribution—a helpful introduction, attendance at an event, sharing of his content—built upon previous ones, creating a pattern of support that had far more impact than any single grand gesture could have achieved.

The Corporate-to-Community Value Bridge

One of my most effective value-leading strategies has been creating connections between corporate executives and community leaders, entrepreneurs, or influencers who would otherwise never meet. This bridge-building creates exponential value by connecting worlds that operate in parallel but rarely intersect.

CHAPTER 2: THE FIRST RULE OF NETWORKING: LEADING WITH VALUE

The idea for my first corporate-community dinner came after noticing how corporate executives often struggled to understand emerging market trends and cultural shifts, while community influencers and entrepreneurs lacked access to corporate resources and expertise. By bringing these groups together in a structured, but relaxed setting, I could create value for everyone involved.

At our first dinner in Atlanta, I seated Marcus, a senior banking executive, next to James, a successful community entrepreneur who had built a thriving urban fashion brand. Initially, they seemed to have little in common. But as the conversation developed, Marcus gained invaluable insights into emerging consumer trends that weren't visible in his corporate reports, while James received practical advice on scaling operations and managing growth.

> **CONNECTION GEM:** *Finding ways to connect different worlds creates exponential value. Look for opportunities to build bridges between groups that could benefit from each other's perspectives.*

What made these dinners particularly valuable was the careful curation of guests and thoughtful facilitation of interactions. I didn't just invite random corporate and community representatives; I strategically selected people whose experiences, challenges, or interests had potential connection points. I also created conversation prompts that would highlight these synergies and make valuable exchanges more likely.

For corporate executives, these dinners provided fresh perspectives from outside their usual spheres of influence. They gained connections to cultural trends and insights that helped them understand emerging markets. They encountered innovative thinking that challenged their established approaches and discovered potential partnership opportunities they would never have found through traditional channels.

Community leaders and entrepreneurs, meanwhile, gained access to business expertise and resources that could help them scale their efforts. They built relationships that sometimes led to corporate sponsorship or support for their initiatives. Their professional networks expanded dramatically, and they received structured business guidance that accelerated their growth.

These value bridges didn't just benefit the participants; they created ripple effects that extended to their organizations and communities. Corporate insights informed more relevant products and services, while community initiatives gained the resources to expand their impact.

Avoiding the Transactional Trap

While value-leading often results in reciprocal benefits, it's important to avoid a purely transactional mindset that can undermine the authenticity and effectiveness of this approach.

I learned this lesson through observing Thomas, a consultant in my industry known for his strategic networking. He meticulously tracked every favor, introduction, or resource he provided, clearly expecting immediate returns on these "investments." While he built an extensive contact list, he developed few genuine relationships and found diminishing responses to his overtures over time.

The transactional trap reveals itself through several telltale signs. Immediate expectation—looking for direct and prompt return on every helpful act—creates an uncomfortable sense of obligation rather than authentic connection. Calculated giving—helping only those who appear positioned to help back—limits relationships to a narrow set of seemingly "useful" individuals, missing the broader value of diverse connections.

> **CONNECTION GEM:** *The moment value-leading becomes transactional, it loses much of its power. Focus on genuine service rather than calculated exchange.*

Value tracking—keeping mental or literal score of giving versus receiving—shifts focus from relationship building to accounting. This scorekeeping mindset inevitably creates resentment when the perceived balance tips one way or the other. Similarly, relationship evaluation based primarily on tangible benefits leads to connections that feel hollow and ultimately unsatisfying.

Perhaps most damaging is conditional support—offering help only with strings attached or clear expectations of return. This approach is typically transparent to recipients, who recognize the difference between genuine assistance and calculated positioning.

The opposite of transactional networking isn't blind generosity—it's service with intention. When you give without keeping score, you create a network built on trust, goodwill, and real connection—not obligation.

This approach doesn't mean never receiving value in return. In fact, the opposite is true—genuinely service-oriented networking typically generates far more reciprocal value over time than direct transactional approaches. The difference lies in the intention and expectation—focusing first on contribution rather than return, and allowing reciprocity to develop naturally through relationship rather than demanding it as payment.

Chapter Takeaways

1. Leading with value immediately sets you apart from 90% of networkers.
2. Different types of value work in different contexts and relationships.
3. Consistency and patience matter more than grand gestures.
4. Bridge-building between different worlds creates exponential value.
5. Knowledge sharing is a powerful form of value-leading.
6. Strategic introductions create value for multiple parties.

7. Avoiding transactional thinking enhances authentic connection.

Action Steps

1. **Conduct a Personal Value Audit**
   - ☐ List your knowledge, skills, connections, and resources.
   - ☐ Identify your unique forms of value.
   - ☐ Connect these to the needs in your network.
2. **Develop Value-Leading Habits**
   - ☐ Create a regular resource-sharing practice.
   - ☐ Set reminders for consistent check-ins.
   - ☐ Build a system for making meaningful introductions.
   - ☐ Establish follow-up routines.
3. **Build Value-Based Networking Scripts**
   - ☐ Develop opening questions focused on others' needs.
   - ☐ Create effective language for offering help.
   - ☐ Practice articulating value in introductions.
   - ☐ Design follow-up templates centered on value.
4. **Create Value Bridges**
   - ☐ Identify different groups in your network.
   - ☐ Look for potential connection points.

- [ ] Plan structured opportunities for cross-group networking.
- [ ] Develop clear value propositions for different groups.

5. **Practice Digital Value-Leading**
   - [ ] Create a content-sharing strategy.
   - [ ] Develop a system for virtual introductions.
   - [ ] Build a digital resource library for sharing.
   - [ ] Establish consistent online engagement practices.

As you incorporate value-leading into your networking approach, you'll find that it not only creates stronger connections but also transforms how you view relationships altogether. Rather than seeing networking as a necessary professional activity, you'll begin to experience it as a meaningful opportunity to create a positive impact.

In the next chapter, we'll explore how to follow through on the connections you create through value-leading, ensuring that initial positive impressions develop into lasting, powerful relationships.

> **Final Connection Gem:** *When value-leading becomes your default approach to relationships, networking transforms from a self-serving activity into a form of service. This shift not only makes you more effective but also more fulfilled in your connections.*

CHAPTER 3

The Art of the Follow-Through

"The fortune is in the follow-up. Relationships are built not in the first meeting, but in the consistent connections that follow. So many networking opportunities are lost because people did not follow up."

At a buzzing networking event in Atlanta, handshakes were firm, smiles wide, and promises to 'stay in touch' floated across the room. Business cards were exchanged, LinkedIn connections clicked, and for a moment, it all felt productive. But I knew the reality—80% of these connections would lead nowhere. The enthusiasm would fade, emails would go unsent, and opportunities would be lost.

The reason? Lack of follow-through.

I've seen this pattern play out countless times throughout my career. People meet, they connect, they express genuine interest in maintaining contact—and then nothing happens. The business cards collect dust, the LinkedIn connections remain dormant, and the relationship potential dissolves into missed opportunities.

This chapter explores what I consider the make-or-break element of powerful networking: consistent, meaningful follow-through. While leading with value gets you in the door, it's follow-through that builds the house. Let's explore how to master this crucial skill.

The Immediate Follow-Up: 24-48 Hour Window

Hours after the conference ended, Lauren, a potential client, received an email from me. While most attendees were still recovering from the networking marathon, I was already in follow-up mode. "It was great meeting you yesterday," I wrote. "Your comments about the challenges of digital transformation in traditional industries really resonated with me. I'm attaching that case study I mentioned about the manufacturing company that successfully navigated this transition. If you'd like to continue the conversation, I'd be happy to schedule a call next Tuesday or Wednesday afternoon."

Lauren responded within the hour: "I'm impressed! Most people say they'll send something, but it rarely happens. This case study looks exactly like what I've been looking for. Wednesday at 2 would work perfectly."

This interaction highlights why the first 24-48 hours after initial contact is the most critical period for follow-through. This narrow window sets the tone for the entire relationship. My timely response demonstrated reliability and genuine interest. The personal reference to our specific conversation made the follow-up feel authentic rather than generic. Providing the promised case study added immediate value, while suggesting specific times for our next conversation created clear next steps.

> **CONNECTION GEM:** *The first follow-up establishes your reliability. Make it prompt, personal, and valuable to set a positive precedent for the relationship.*

This immediate follow-up did more than just continue our conversation—it differentiated me from the dozens of other connections Lauren had made at the conference. In a sea of good intentions and unfulfilled promises to "keep in touch," concrete, timely action stands out dramatically.

I've found that this 24-48 hour window is non-negotiable for important connections. Even when traveling or extremely busy, I prioritize these immediate follow-ups, often drafting them on flights or during brief breaks. The impression made during this critical window can accelerate relationship development by months or create opportunities that would otherwise never materialize.

Creating Follow-Through Systems

I didn't always have a strong follow-up system. Early in my career, I relied on memory and good intentions—which, unsurprisingly, failed me. Emails were forgotten, business cards piled up, and promising connections slipped through the cracks.

Everything changed when I met Sophia, a seasoned executive who seemed to maintain hundreds of meaningful relationships effortlessly. When I asked about her secret, she laughed. "It's not magic; it's systems," she explained. "Without them, I'd be just as scattered as everyone else."

Inspired by Sophia, I developed my own relationship management system. I started with a simple contact database that included not just basic information, but notes about conversations, personal details, and potential value I could offer each connection. I blocked specific times in my calendar devoted exclusively to follow-up activities—Monday mornings for new connections, Friday afternoons for relationship maintenance. I also stored people's contacts in my phone with the place I met them and their company, which helps me remember them.

I created a reminder structure that prompted me when to reach out to different tiers of contacts, ensuring no important relationship went too long without attention. I organized my content—articles, resources, and opportunities—in a way that made it easy to share relevant information with specific connections. And I developed customizable communication templates that I could quickly personalize for different follow-up scenarios.

> **CONNECTION GEM:** *Systems free your mind to focus on relationship quality rather than remembering details. Even simple systems dramatically improve follow-through consistency.*

These systems transformed my networking effectiveness. Instead of worrying about remembering to follow up, I could focus on the quality of each interaction. Rather than frantically searching for that business card from last week's event, I had all the information at my fingertips. The systems handled the logistics so I could concentrate on the human connection.

What I learned from this experience is that consistent follow-through isn't a function of memory or even discipline—it's a function of effective systems. Even simple structures dramatically improve connection consistency and depth.

The Follow-Through Timeline

My relationship with David, who eventually became both a client and a friend, illustrates how different stages of relationship development require different follow-through approaches.

After meeting David at an industry panel, I sent a personalized email the next morning. "I enjoyed our conversation about content marketing challenges for B2B companies," I wrote. "Here's that podcast episode I mentioned that addresses the measurement issues you described. I'd love to continue our discussion—perhaps over coffee next week if your schedule permits?"

This initial follow-up within 24 hours included a specific reference to our conversation, provided a valuable resource, suggested a clear next step, and maintained a personal tone that reflected our actual interaction.

Two weeks later, after our coffee meeting, I sent a secondary follow-up: "Great speaking with you last week. I came across this new research on B2B content engagement metrics that might help with the tracking challenges you mentioned. How has your team's exploration of the new analytics platform been going? Also, I'm moderating a panel on this exact topic next month—I'd be happy to add your name to the guest list if you're interested."

This secondary follow-up maintained connection without pressure, provided additional relevant resources, expressed curiosity about his progress, shared a potential opportunity, and continued building our relationship on both professional and personal levels.

> **CONNECTION GEM:** *Different relationship stages require different follow-through approaches. Customize your follow-through strategy based on the relationship development stage.*

In the months that followed, I established regular maintenance contact with David. These quarterly check-ins recognized his company's achievements, shared information specific to his expressed interests, included authentic updates about my own professional journey, and gradually deepened our connection beyond strictly business topics.

This timeline approach—immediate follow-up, secondary connection within two weeks, and regular maintenance thereafter—provided a structural framework for our evolving relationship. The frequency and depth of contact naturally evolved as our connection developed, but the consistent presence maintained the momentum that turned a casual meeting into a valuable long-term relationship.

Follow-Through Communication Strategies

The content of your follow-through communications significantly impacts its effectiveness. I learned this by comparing approaches with my colleague Robert, who was great at follow-up—in theory. He sent emails on time, but they were generic, long-winded, and focused on what he needed. No personalization. No clear purpose. No real connection.

His response rate? Almost zero.

When we sat down to fix it, I gave him a few simple tweaks:

- Personalize it—reference a specific detail from your last conversation.

- Keep it short—no one has time for paragraphs.
- Make it about them—offer something valuable before asking for anything.

He put it into practice, and the change was immediate. His responses doubled, and conversations became real relationships.

I shared with Robert some of the communication strategies I had developed for more effective follow-through. I showed him how I personalized each interaction with specific references to previous conversations or the recipient's work. I demonstrated the power of brevity—respecting people's time through concise, focused messages. I explained the importance of clarity about intentions and any requests, making it easy for people to respond appropriately.

> **CONNECTION GEM:** *Follow-through communication should balance professionalism with personality. Be efficient without sacrificing the human element that builds real connection.*

Most importantly, I emphasized maintaining a value focus—ensuring each communication offered something beneficial to the recipient rather than just making requests. I stressed the importance of authenticity—maintaining a genuine voice and approach that reflected my actual personality rather than an overly formal or artificial "networking" persona.

Robert adjusted his approach based on these principles, and the results were dramatic. His response rates increased substantially, and his follow-up conversations became much more engaging and productive. "I realize now that I was so focused on the act of following up that I wasn't thinking enough about the quality of the communication," he told me. "The same time investment with a better approach is yielding completely different results."

The Art of Rekindling Dormant Connections

Even with the best intentions, some connections go dormant. The ability to effectively rekindle these relationships is a valuable skill I've developed through both success and failure in reconnection efforts.

Some connections fade—not out of conflict, but out of life happening. That was the case with a close contact of mine. Two years of silence. No falling-out, just busy schedules. I almost let it go, but then I asked myself: What if one email could bring this relationship back?

I sent a simple message:

"It's been too long! I was just thinking about our last conversation on AI in healthcare, and I came across this article—I think you'd love it. I would love to catch up when you're free."

The response? Instant. "I was just thinking about you! Let's grab coffee next week."

One email. One thoughtful moment. Relationship restored.

My approach began with authentic acknowledgment of the gap. "It's been far too long since we've been in touch," I wrote. "I've missed our conversations and the insights you always shared so generously." This honesty about the lapsed connection was far more effective than pretending the gap hadn't occurred.

Following my value-first philosophy, I included something helpful in this reconnection attempt—an article directly relevant to a project I knew he had been working on when we last spoke. This demonstrated that my outreach was about giving rather than asking, making the reconnection attempt feel like an offer rather than a request.

> **CONNECTION GEM:** *It's almost never too late to rekindle valuable connections. Most people respond positively to authentic reconnection efforts, especially when approached with value rather than need.*

I maintained a non-demanding tone throughout my message, making it clear that I wasn't placing pressure or obligation on him to respond. "I'd love to hear how you've been and what you're working on now, if you have the time and interest to reconnect," I wrote, creating space for him to engage at his comfort level.

I provided relevant context for my outreach, explaining what had prompted me to think of him and reach out now. "I've recently been working on a project involving AI applications in healthcare, which reminded me of your pioneering work in this area," I explained, making the reconnection feel meaningful rather than random.

My message focused on the future rather than dwelling too much on the past lapse in communication. "I'd love to catch up and explore ways we might collaborate or support each other's work going forward," I suggested, creating a forward-looking framework for renewed connection.

The response was immediate and enthusiastic. "I was just thinking about you last week!" he replied. "This article is perfect timing for my current project. Let's definitely reconnect—how about coffee next Tuesday?"

This experience taught me that most people are open to rekindling valuable connections, especially when approached with authenticity and value rather than need or obligation. The key is making the reconnection process as comfortable and beneficial as possible for the other person.

Chapter Takeaways

1. The first 24-48 hours after initial contact set the tone for relationship development.
2. Effective follow-through requires systems, not just good intentions.

3. Different relationship stages need different follow-through approaches.
4. Small daily follow-through habits create compound returns over time.
5. Match your communication platform to the relationship stage.
6. As your network grows, prioritize connections rather than attempting equal depth with everyone.
7. It's rarely too late to rekindle valuable dormant connections.

Action Steps

1. **Create Your Follow-Through System**
   - ☐ Choose a contact management approach.
   - ☐ Establish regular follow-up time blocks.
   - ☐ Develop customizable templates.
   - ☐ Set up reminder systems.
2. **Implement the 24-Hour Rule**
   - ☐ Commit to following up within 24 hours of new connections.
   - ☐ Create a standard first follow-up approach.
   - ☐ Prepare shareable resources for immediate value.
3. **Develop Platform Strategies**
   - ☐ Identify your primary follow-through platforms.

- ☐ Create different approaches for different channels.
- ☐ Build a content-sharing system.

4. **Build a Relationship Maintenance Calendar**
   - ☐ Schedule regular check-ins with key connections.
   - ☐ Create different schedules for different relationship types.
   - ☐ Set reminders for significant dates and events.

5. **Practice Rekindling Skills**
   - ☐ Identify 3-5 dormant, but potentially valuable connections.
   - ☐ Create personalized rekindling messages.
   - ☐ Reach out with a value-first approach.

CHAPTER 4

Breaking Bread, Breaking Barriers

"Breaking bread breaks down barriers. There's something about sharing a meal that allows connections to form more naturally and deeply than any boardroom ever could."

In an elegant private dining room, New York's corporate executives and entertainment industry leaders shared a meal and exchanged ideas, insights, and opportunities. A senior banking executive debated marketing trends with a Grammy-nominated artist. A tech entrepreneur and a film producer explored digital distribution models. At the head of the table, the mayor leaned in, captivated by a community organizer's vision for neighborhood development.

This went beyond dinner. This was connection in its purest form.

This gathering was intentional. It wasn't just about food; it was about building bridges between worlds that rarely intersected. Over the years, I've learned that some of the most valuable professional connections don't happen in boardrooms—they happen over dinner tables.

Breaking bread breaks down barriers.

The phrase "breaking bread" has ancient origins across many cultures, and for good reason. There's something fundamentally human about sharing food that creates psychological safety, fosters authentic communication, and breaks down the invisible barriers that often separate us in professional settings.

In this chapter, we'll explore how to use this timeless connection strategy in modern professional contexts—from intimate coffee meetings to strategic dinner gatherings to vision board brunches. I'll share specific approaches for creating gatherings that transform disconnected individuals into powerful networks and turn separate worlds into collaborative communities.

The Psychology of Shared Meals

Early in my career, I hosted a dinner where two executives, locked in a tense negotiation, sat stiffly across from each other—arms crossed, avoiding eye contact. The tension was thick.

Then, something shifted. As the meal progressed, they passed dishes, found common ground, and by dessert, they were laughing over their kids' sports teams. Two weeks later, they struck a deal that had once seemed impossible.

Why? Because food isn't just fuel—it's a connector.

The business matter wasn't resolved that evening, but the relationship fundamentally changed. Two weeks later, they reached an agreement that had seemed impossible before that dinner.

This transformation wasn't just cultural conditioning—it was rooted in human psychology and biology. When we share food, our bodies actually release oxytocin, the same "bonding hormone" active in close relationships. The act of eating together creates a subtle vulnerability we all share, breaking down barriers through this common experience. The natural pacing of a meal—from appetizers through dessert—creates a conversation flow that builds gradually rather than forcing immediate depth.

> **CONNECTION GEM:** *The power of shared meals isn't just cultural tradition—it's rooted in human psychology. When we eat together, physiological and psychological processes naturally create connection.*

The sensory experience of shared food—the tastes, smells, and visual presentation we all enjoy simultaneously—builds emotional connection through these common reference points. Perhaps most interestingly, sharing a meal temporarily reduces hierarchical barriers. When everyone at the table is engaged in the same basic human activity of eating, status differences naturally diminish, creating more authentic conversation.

Understanding these psychological principles helps explain why breaking bread has remained a fundamental connection strategy across cultures and throughout history. It's not just tradition—it's a practice aligned with our deepest human wiring for building relationships.

My Breaking Bread Journey

My love for bringing people together over food didn't start in boardrooms—it started at home. Sunday dinners were intentional. No matter how busy we were, we gathered around the table, sharing stories, debating ideas, and strengthening bonds. My mother's ability to use these gatherings to maintain family bonds, share important information, and create community left a lasting impression.

I vividly remember how these dinners transcended simple meals. Neighbors would stop by, relatives would visit, and conversations would flow naturally from lighthearted stories to deeper discussions about community needs, family challenges, and shared dreams. My mother instinctively understood that food created a foundation for connection that mere meetings couldn't match.

Years later, when I moved to Atlanta and began building new professional networks, I instinctively turned to food as a connection tool. What began as casual dinners with my friends from different industries evolved into strategic gatherings bringing together diverse professionals and industry leaders who might never otherwise connect. The conversation that night revealed collaboration opportunities we'd never discovered. This experience sparked a realization—I could deliberately use shared meals to create valuable connections in my expanding professional and personal world.

> **CONNECTION GEM:** *Your earliest experiences with connection often shape your approach to professional relationship building. Recognize and leverage these intuitive patterns rather than abandoning them for more "professional" networking approaches.*

Over time, these informal gatherings evolved into more strategic events, eventually becoming signature experiences that defined my professional identity as The Master Connector. Yet the fundamental approach remained rooted in those early family dinners—creating spaces where food serves as both nourishment and a social catalyst, where conversation can develop organically, and where relationships build through shared experience rather than transactional networking.

Case Study: The Corporate-Creative Dinner Series

Corporate executives and creative leaders often operate in the same city—but in different worlds. I saw an opportunity.

I launched a quarterly dinner series where these industries could connect in a way that felt natural, not forced. Executives gained fresh cultural insights; creatives found potential partners. Conversations flowed, collaborations formed, and barriers disappeared.

The initial concept emerged from conversations with both corporate and creative leaders who expressed curiosity about the other's world but had no natural connection points. My first attempt was modest—a small dinner with five executives and five successful business owners at a local small restaurant. The conversation that night revealed fascinating synergies—the executives gained fresh perspectives on consumer trends and creative approaches to business challenges, while the creative leaders gained insights into business operations and potential corporate partnerships.

Encouraged by this success, I refined the format based on participant feedback. The ideal group size emerged as eight to ten people, evenly split between sectors. The most effective structure included brief introductions highlighting current projects or challenges, followed by an open but gently guided conversation during the meal, and concluding with explicit connection opportunities for follow-up.

As word spread about these gatherings, demand for participation grew. Rather than simply expanding the size—which would have diminished the quality of the intimate conversation—I maintained the small format but increased frequency, eventually establishing a regular cadence of quarterly dinners. Each gathering maintained the crucial balance between corporate and creative worlds, ensuring mutual value for all participants.

> **CONNECTION GEM:** *Creating signature gathering experiences that become known within your network significantly enhances your connector reputation and creates ongoing connection opportunities.*

The key strategic elements that made these dinners successful went beyond basic hospitality. The balanced curation ensured equal representation and status between different sectors, preventing either world from dominating. The structured informality—enough organization to ensure purposeful connection while allowing natural conversation flow—created an experience that felt organic despite careful planning.

Clear value propositions for all participants made these gatherings attractive to busy professionals. Corporate executives gained fresh creative perspectives and cultural insights, while creative leaders gained business wisdom and potential partnership opportunities. Each participant could identify specific potential value before even arriving.

My personal hosting presence throughout the event—from thoughtful introductions to subtle conversation guidance to post-event follow-up—ensured the gathering achieved its connection potential rather than devolving into standard networking or social conversation. And the consistent quarterly cadence created anticipation and continuity, building a recognizable community around these gatherings rather than isolated events.

The impact of this dinner series extended far beyond the actual evenings. Business partnerships formed, creative projects found funding, and perhaps most valuably, ongoing relationships developed between worlds that had previously existed separately despite geographic proximity. What began as an experimental dinner became a signature connection strategy that defined my professional reputation in both communities.

The Vision Board Brunch: Personal-Professional Connection

Some gatherings build careers. Others build dreams.

That's why I host Vision Board Brunches every year—a space where personal and professional aspirations merge. Over breakfast, we cut, paste, and craft visual roadmaps for the future. But the real magic? The shared vulnerability of saying dreams out loud—and watching them come true.

The concept emerged somewhat accidentally. Five years ago, I invited a few close professional friends to my home for New Year's brunch and suggested we might create vision boards together for the coming year. What began as a casual gathering revealed unprecedented connection depth as we shared not just professional goals but personal aspirations, challenges, and dreams while creating visual representations of the year ahead.

These brunches have since evolved into one of my most popular and impactful gathering traditions. The goal-setting focus creates natural depth as participants share their visualized plans for the coming year. Unlike purely professional events where personal aspects remain hidden, these gatherings create space for whole-person connection, revealing shared interests and values that might never emerge in standard business contexts.

The supportive environment that develops through shared creativity and goal-sharing naturally builds stronger bonds than typical networking. As participants help each other find images or words representing specific goals, they demonstrate support in tangible ways. This collaborative atmosphere continues as people share their completed boards, often receiving encouragement and specific offers of help from others in the group.

> **CONNECTION GEM:** *Gatherings that blend personal and professional elements often create deeper, more lasting connections than purely business-focused events.*

Resource sharing happens organically as participants discover each other's goals. When James mentioned his vision to publish his first book, Sarah immediately offered to introduce him to her editor. When Renee shared her plan to run her first marathon, Thomas connected her with his running group. These immediate value exchanges emerge naturally from the vision-sharing context.

Perhaps most valuably, these brunches create accountability structures that extend beyond the gathering itself. The shared goals and public declarations naturally lead to follow-up conversations throughout the year. "How's your house search going?" or "Did you launch that new service yet?" become natural check-in points that maintain connection long after the event.

The community-building aspect of these brunches has created a distinct connection group that has evolved over the years. Participants now reach out to each other independently, creating a web of relationships that functions as an ongoing support network rather than just event-based connections.

The vision board brunch concept demonstrates how breaking bread can create deeper connections when combined with activities that encourage meaningful sharing. The combination of food's natural connection power with purposeful creative activity generates relationships that blend professional value with personal authenticity.

The Post-Meal Connection Continuation

What happens after breaking bread often determines long-term connection value, as I've observed through relationships that either flourished or faded following shared meals.

I used to think hosting a great dinner was enough. It's not.

The real work starts after the meal ends. Without follow-up, connections fade. The best hosts don't just bring people together—they help keep them connected.

Expression of appreciation provides the foundation for effective post-gathering connection. After a recent strategic dinner, I sent personalized messages to each participant within 24 hours, expressing specific gratitude for their contribution to the gathering. These weren't generic thank-you notes, but thoughtful acknowledgments mentioning particular insights shared or connections made. This immediate follow-up maintained the connection momentum established during the meal.

> **CONNECTION GEM:** *Breaking bread initiates connection, but follow-through transforms it into lasting relationship value. Always have a post-gathering connection strategy.*

Highlight sharing extends this appreciation approach by noting specific valuable moments from the gathering. In my follow-up with participants from a cross-industry dinner, I mentioned particular conversation insights I found valuable: "Your perspective on community engagement strategies provided a fresh approach that several of us hadn't considered." This specific acknowledgment both affirmed their contributions and anchored the connection to a concrete shared experience.

Connection facilitation through introduction follow-through transforms initial interest into an ongoing relationship. When two participants at my entrepreneurial dinner expressed mutual interest in potential collaboration, I facilitated their continued connection through a direct email introduction the following day, providing context from our shared meal experience. This active facilitation moved the relationship beyond the gathering itself into independent development.

Resource provision after breaking bread creates additional value that strengthens new connections. Following a discussion of marketing challenges during a recent industry dinner, I shared relevant articles, tool recommendations, and case studies with participants who had expressed interest in this topic. This resource sharing extended the gathering's value while demonstrating ongoing support for their professional concerns.

Next gathering planning creates a continuation expectation that maintains connection between meals. At the conclusion of quarterly industry dinners, I always mention the date of the next gathering, creating anticipation for ongoing community participation rather than experiencing each dinner as an isolated event.

This continuation framing helps relationships develop through multiple touchpoints rather than single interactions.

This thoughtful post-meal nurturing transforms what might be pleasant but isolated social experiences into the foundation for ongoing valuable relationships. The breaking bread experience creates initial connection potential, but it's the subsequent follow-through that develops this potential into meaningful professional relationships.

Chapter Takeaways

1. Shared meals create psychological safety that facilitates deeper connection.
2. Different breaking bread formats serve different relationship-building purposes.
3. Effective gatherings require thoughtful curation and facilitation.
4. Creating memorable food experiences builds lasting relationship anchors.
5. Breaking bread naturally bridges hierarchical, cultural, and professional boundaries.
6. The host mindset goes beyond logistics to create emotional connection experiences.
7. Follow-through transforms breaking bread moments into lasting relationship value

Action Steps

1. **Develop Your Breaking Bread Strategy**
   - ☐ Identify your gathering purpose and approach.
   - ☐ Select appropriate formats for your goals.
   - ☐ Create your signature gathering elements.
   - ☐ Build your host capabilities.

2. **Create Your Gathering Framework**
   - ☐ Develop a guest curation approach.
   - ☐ Build conversation facilitation tools.
   - ☐ Design environment and experience elements
   - ☐ Establish follow-through systems.

3. **Build Your Hospitality Toolkit**
   - ☐ Identify suitable venues for different gathering types.
   - ☐ Develop relationships with key hospitality partners.
   - ☐ Create a resource collection for gathering elements.
   - ☐ Establish budget frameworks for different approaches.

4. **Enhance Your Host Abilities**
   - ☐ Practice conversation facilitation techniques.
   - ☐ Develop welcome and inclusion strategies.
   - ☐ Create connection-spotting abilities.
   - ☐ Build memory-creating capabilities.

CHAPTER 4: BREAKING BREAD, BREAKING BARRIERS

5. **Implement Regular Gathering Rhythms**
   - ☐ Establish a consistent connection meal cadence.
   - ☐ Create annual signature events.
   - ☐ Build gathering tradition elements.
   - ☐ Develop a gathering evolution approach.

In a digital age where formal business interactions often dominate, breaking bread together creates a rare space for human connection that transcends professional roles. Your ability to create these moments of authentic connection through shared meals will become one of your most valuable relationship-building assets.

In the next chapter, we'll explore how to bridge cultural and professional gaps, creating valuable connections between different worlds.

> **Final Connection Gem:** *Business happens in boardrooms. But real relationships? They're built over dinner tables. Master the art of breaking bread, and you'll master the art of connection.*

CHAPTER 5

Bridging Different Worlds

> *"The most valuable connections often come from bridging worlds that rarely intersect. When you build bridges between different worlds, you create opportunities that others can't even see."*

The tension in the room was palpable. On one side sat executives from a top financial institution, fluent in metrics, market share, and investment strategies. Across from them were community leaders from underserved Atlanta neighborhoods, focused on housing displacement, economic survival, and rebuilding trust.

Though just miles apart, these two groups lived in different realities. And now, they had to find common ground.

Bridging these worlds wasn't just about translating words—it was about translating values.

The banking executives spoke of "market penetration," "customer acquisition costs," and "brand positioning." The community leaders discussed "displacement concerns," "economic empowerment," and "authentic engagement." Though they shared a genuine desire to create a positive impact, their communication patterns created invisible barriers to effective collaboration.

This scenario highlights one of the most valuable skills a master connector can develop: the ability to bridge cultural and professional gaps. The most valuable relationships aren't always formed within industries or peer circles. They happen when you build bridges between worlds that rarely intersect. Throughout my career, I've found myself acting as a translator between different worlds—inner city and Wall Street, corporate and creative, academic and entrepreneurial. This ability to move authentically between different environments has created extraordinary value, allowing me to build connections that others cannot.

In this chapter, we'll explore the art and science of bridging these gaps—how to understand, navigate, and connect different cultural and professional worlds in ways that create value for everyone involved.

Understanding Cultural and Professional Gaps

My first real lesson in gap-bridging came during my initial weeks on Wall Street. In a meeting with senior traders, I used terminology from my economics courses at Virginia Union University that, while academically correct, didn't match the trading floor vernacular. The subtle looks exchanged around the table made it clear I was speaking the wrong "language" despite being technically accurate.

Later, a mentor pulled me aside. "You need to understand that each world has its own dialect," he explained. "Academic finance, trading floor operations, client presentations—they all use different terms for the same concepts. Your job is to learn to translate between them."

This experience taught me to recognize the various types of gaps that can separate people who might otherwise connect powerfully.

Bridging gaps starts with understanding them:

1. Cultural gaps: Differences in values, norms, and communication styles.
2. Professional gaps: Industry-specific language and priorities.
3. Socioeconomic gaps: Varying economic experiences and opportunities.
4. Educational gaps: Different levels of academic exposure and training.
5. Generational gaps: Contrasting mindsets shaped by age and experience.

> **CONNECTION GEM:** *Each type of gap requires different bridging strategies. The first step in effective bridge-building is accurately identifying which gaps are present in a specific situation.*

The key insight was that recognizing which specific gaps exist in a given situation allows you to apply appropriate bridging strategies rather than using a one-size-fits-all approach that might miss the actual barriers preventing connection.

The Bridge-Builder Mindset

What truly transformed my ability to connect different worlds was adopting what I now call the "bridge-builder mindset." This perspective shift happened during a project connecting corporate retailers with urban fashion entrepreneurs.

At first, I found myself stuck between two sides—defending the entrepreneurs when executives dismissed their unpolished pitches and then rationalizing corporate constraints when the entrepreneurs grew frustrated.

Then it clicked.

I wasn't supposed to take sides. I was supposed to build the bridge.

Instead of choosing a camp, I focused on translating value: "What the executives mean by 'scalable processes' is..." or "When the designers talk about 'authentic expression,' they're referring to..."

That's when real connections started happening. This back-and-forth advocacy was well-intentioned but ultimately ineffective.

The breakthrough came when I stopped seeing myself as representing either side and began viewing my role as a translator between worlds. Rather than defending positions, I focused on helping each group understand the other's perspective. "What the executives mean by 'scalable processes' is..." or "When the designers talk about 'authentic expression,' they're referring to..."

> **CONNECTION GEM:** *Bridge-building begins with mindset. When you see yourself as a translator between worlds rather than a representative of one side, you naturally look for connection points that others miss.*

This translator mindset requires genuine curiosity about different perspectives, suspending judgment while seeking understanding. It involves pattern recognition—identifying similarities beneath surface differences—and value appreciation for different approaches. Most importantly, it requires a translation orientation, seeing yourself fundamentally as an interpreter between worlds rather than an advocate for one side.

My Journey as a Bridge-Builder

My perspective on bridging gaps developed through navigating multiple worlds throughout my life and career. Growing up in

Newark's inner-city neighborhoods and later working on Wall Street trading floors taught me to translate between environments that rarely intersected despite their geographic proximity.

The transition from Virginia Union University, a historically Black college, to investment banking culture required learning entirely new social codes while maintaining an authentic connection to my identity and background. Moving from New York's direct, fast-paced business culture to Atlanta's relationship-focused approach necessitated regional adaptation while maintaining professional effectiveness.

Perhaps most significantly, shifting from corporate environments to entrepreneurial settings required translating between employed and self-employed worlds with fundamentally different perspectives on risk, opportunity, and success. Building connections between financial institutions and creative industries highlighted how professional cultures that could benefit from collaboration often remain separated by communication differences.

> **CONNECTION GEM:** *Your personal journey between different environments gives you unique bridge-building capabilities. The transitions you've navigated—whether cultural, professional, or socioeconomic—provide a valuable perspective for connecting different worlds.*

These experiences taught me that effective bridge-building isn't just about understanding different environments superficially, but developing a deep appreciation for their values, priorities, and perspectives. The most valuable skill became the ability to translate value between these worlds—helping each side understand what the other offers and how collaboration could create mutual benefit beyond what either could achieve independently.

Strategies for Building Communication Bridges

One of the most transformative techniques I've developed is value translation—explicitly helping different groups recognize mutual benefit potential that might otherwise remain invisible. During a project connecting financial institutions with creative entrepreneurs, I created "value maps" that showed specifically how each group's capabilities addressed the other's challenges. These visual representations helped everyone see collaboration potential beyond immediate differences.

Terminology bridging provides another powerful technique. When working with technologists and non-technical business leaders, I developed a shared lexicon that captured essential technical concepts without specialized jargon. This "translation dictionary" allowed for productive conversation without requiring either group to fully adopt the other's specialized language.

> **CONNECTION GEM:** *Developing specific communication tools for bridging different worlds creates exponential value. Even simple translation mechanisms can transform previously impossible collaborations into productive partnerships.*

Context provision helps establish shared understanding across different perspectives. When facilitating interactions between corporate executives and community organizations, I created brief orientation materials for both groups—helping executives understand community history and priorities while giving community leaders insight into corporate decision-making constraints. This mutual context established the foundation for more productive engagement.

Perhaps most powerfully, perspective exchange creates authentic understanding beyond abstract knowledge. When connecting different professional worlds, I use carefully structured activities where participants temporarily adopt each other's perspectives and attempt to articulate problems from that viewpoint. These exchanges develop empathy and appreciation that transform subsequent interactions.

The Ethics of Cultural Bridge-Building

Respectful gap-bridging requires thoughtful ethical navigation to ensure connections create mutual benefit rather than exploit differences. I learned this through observing contrasting approaches to cross-cultural engagement throughout my career.

Some connectors approached cultural bridge-building primarily as an opportunity for personal advantage—adopting superficial cultural elements that created the appearance of connection without genuine understanding or respect. While sometimes temporarily effective for specific transactions, this approach inevitably created damaged relationships and diminished reputation over time.

Ethical bridge-building goes beyond learning just enough to blend in—it's about deep understanding.

Superficial connections might open doors temporarily, but real credibility comes from true engagement. That means taking the time to learn beyond the surface—not just what a community values, but why they value it.

> **CONNECTION GEM:** *If you want lasting relationships, don't just visit the culture—respect it and make sure it is mutually beneficial.*

Appropriate representation means being clear about your perspective and limitations—acknowledging when you're sharing understanding as an outsider rather than claiming insider knowledge. Credit attribution acknowledges sources of cultural knowledge rather than presenting insights as your own discoveries, recognizing the contributions of those who have shared their experience and wisdom.

Exploitation avoidance ensures mutual benefit rather than one-sided advantage in cross-cultural engagement. This means considering how bridge-building activities impact all involved communities, not just your personal or organizational interests. Learning orientation maintains humility and a growth mindset, recognizing that cultural understanding is an ongoing journey rather than a destination to be reached.

These ethical principles enhance rather than constrain effective bridge-building by creating sustainable connections built on authentic respect and mutual value. While requiring more investment than superficial approaches, ethical bridge-building generates lasting relationship capital that creates continuing returns beyond immediate transactions.

Building Your Bridge-Building Skills

Anyone can develop effective bridge-building capabilities through deliberate practice and mindset development. The foundation begins with genuine curiosity about different perspectives, cultures, and approaches. This openness to authentic understanding creates the necessary foundation for effective translation between worlds.

Skills development should include active listening across differences—learning to hear beyond words to understand the underlying values and priorities that shape communication. Cross-cultural communication study—whether through formal education, self-directed learning, or guided exposure—builds an essential knowledge foundation for effective bridging.

> **CONNECTION GEM:** *Bridge-building is both an art and a science. Deliberately developing specific connection capabilities dramatically enhances your ability to create value across different worlds.*

Experience expansion through deliberate exposure to different environments provides invaluable practical understanding beyond theoretical knowledge. Whenever possible, immerse yourself in unfamiliar contexts with guidance from insiders who can help interpret experiences appropriately.

Perhaps most importantly, reflection practice helps integrate bridge-building experiences into deeper understanding. After cross-cultural or cross-professional interactions, deliberately analyze what worked, what created barriers, and how approaches might improve in future engagements.

The most effective bridge-builders maintain consistent development through these practices, recognizing that cultural intelligence and translation capability require ongoing refinement rather than one-time mastery. This continuous learning approach ensures your bridge-building skills remain relevant as cultural and professional contexts evolve.

Chapter Takeaways

1. Bridge-building across cultural and professional gaps creates unique connection value.
2. Effective gap-bridging begins with a translator mindset rather than a representative perspective.
3. Multiple "languages"—both cultural and professional—enhance your connector capabilities.
4. Creating neutral "third spaces" often facilitates more authentic cross-gap connection.
5. Ethical bridge-building ensures mutual benefit rather than one-sided advantage.
6. Bridge-builder reputation creates cumulative connection opportunities.

Action Steps

1. **Conduct a Gap Analysis**
   - ☐ Identify the different worlds you naturally navigate.
   - ☐ Assess your current bridge-building strengths.
   - ☐ Recognize gaps in your connection capabilities.
   - ☐ Evaluate high-value bridging opportunities.
   - ☐ Determine priority development areas.

2. **Develop Your Cultural Intelligence**
   - ☐ Build knowledge about different cultural frameworks.
   - ☐ Enhance awareness of cultural dynamics in interactions.
   - ☐ Practice adapting behavior appropriately.
   - ☐ Cultivate a genuine interest in cultural differences.
   - ☐ Improve skills in interpreting cultural contexts.

3. **Enhance Your Language Portfolio**
   - ☐ Learn terminology across different professional sectors.
   - ☐ Develop translation capabilities between environments.
   - ☐ Practice communication style adaptation.
   - ☐ Build skills in explaining different value frameworks.
   - ☐ Create bridges between specialized languages.

4. **Design Bridge-Building Opportunities**
   - ☐ Create "third space" connection environments.
   - ☐ Develop cross-cultural/professional gatherings.
   - ☐ Build opportunities for diverse group interaction.

- ☐ Establish neutral territory for authentic engagement.
- ☐ Create shared experiences across differences.

5. **Establish Your Ethical Framework**
   - ☐ Define personal bridge-building boundaries.
   - ☐ Create principles for respectful engagement.
   - ☐ Develop mutual benefit approaches.
   - ☐ Build authentic connection strategies.
   - ☐ Establish continuous learning practices.

In a world increasingly divided by specialization, culture, and perspective, bridge-builders create extraordinary value through connection. By developing the ability to move authentically between different environments while helping others do the same, you position yourself not just as a networker but as a creator of new possibilities through meaningful relationship building.

In the next chapter, we'll explore how to invest in access—creating strategic positioning that places you in environments where valuable connections naturally occur.

> **Final Connection Gem:** *Most people network within their world. Bridge-builders connect across worlds. Your ability to translate between cultures, industries, and perspectives won't just expand your network—it will create opportunities no one else can see.*

CHAPTER 6

Investing in Access: Strategic Positioning

"Sometimes you have to invest in being in the right room. The cost of access often pales in comparison to the value of the opportunities you gain."

When my Uncle Derrick heard I had spent $1,600 on a first-class plane ticket from Atlanta to New Jersey for a family emergency, he was shocked. "You're from Newark," he exclaimed. "Put your ghetto behind back in coach! You can meet someone that might want to join your Master Connector community back there."

My response was simple but profound: "But I can meet an investor in first class."

That conversation captures an essential principle of high-level networking that many people miss: strategic investment in access often creates returns that far exceed the initial cost. On that very flight, I met an executive who later became a valuable business advisor, helping me scale The Master Connector Agency in ways that generated far more than the $1,600 first-class ticket price.

This chapter explores the concept of strategic positioning—making intentional investments that place you in environments where valuable connections naturally occur. While authentic relationship building remains the foundation of powerful networking, deliberately positioning yourself in high-opportunity environments dramatically increases your chances of making game-changing connections.

Understanding Access Investment

The concept of investing in access truly crystallized for me during a conversation with Candace, a successful entrepreneur I met at a business conference. Over dinner, she shared how she had initially hesitated to spend $5,000 on a premium mastermind group, viewing it as an extravagant expense she couldn't justify as a startup founder.

"Six months later," she told me, "that investment had generated over $50,000 in new business through relationships I built in that group. What I had seen as an expense was actually an investment with a 10X return."

This perspective shift fundamentally changed my approach to networking resources. Access investment is about positioning yourself where valuable connections naturally happen.

Think about it this way: If you're a musician trying to land a record deal, where are you more likely to meet a major label executive—at a free open-mic night or backstage at the Grammys?

One costs nothing. The other requires strategic investment.

This is the key: Access isn't given—it's created. And sometimes, the best way to create it is by removing the barriers that keep you out of high-value rooms.

> **CONNECTION GEM:** *Access investment isn't about "paying for friends" or buying influence. It's about strategically removing barriers that prevent natural, authentic connections with people in different circles.*

Strategic positioning allows you to place yourself in high-opportunity environments where valuable connections naturally occur. This placement, combined with authentic engagement within these accessed spaces, creates connection possibilities that pure networking effort alone cannot produce. The key is maximizing these opportunities once access is created, maintaining a long-term perspective about the cumulative value of these investments over time.

I've found that many people hesitate to invest in strategic positioning because they view these expenditures purely as costs rather than potential returns. The first-class ticket, the exclusive conference, the premium membership—these are seen as expenses to minimize rather than strategic investments that might yield exponential returns through the relationships they make possible.

The Access Investment Mindset

At first, I saw expensive networking opportunities as luxuries I couldn't afford.

That changed when I faced a tough decision: Should I spend $5,000 on an exclusive Business Leaders cohort? It felt extravagant—until I asked myself a different question:

What if the relationships I build there generate 10X that investment?

I took the leap.

Six months later, that decision led to partnerships that brought in well over six figures. What once seemed like an expense became the best investment I ever made.

Looking strictly at my budget, this seemed like an extravagance I should avoid. But when I reframed the question—"What connections might this environment make possible?"—the decision calculus changed entirely.

CHAPTER 6: INVESTING IN ACCESS: STRATEGIC POSITIONING

The Business Cohort brought together exactly the caliber of industry leaders I hoped to connect with, in an intimate setting designed for relationship building rather than superficial networking. Viewing the fee as an investment in potential relationships rather than merely an expense transformed my perspective. I decided to attend, and the connections made during the 6-month cohort eventually led to partnerships worth many times the initial investment.

> **CONNECTION GEM:** *The shift from seeing networking costs as expenses to viewing them as investments fundamentally changes your approach. This perspective transforms how you evaluate everything from conference fees to travel costs.*

This opportunity perspective—seeing potential returns rather than just immediate costs—represents the foundation of the access investment mindset. Combined with clear value recognition for certain high-opportunity environments, this approach moves you from scarcity thinking to an abundance perspective about connection possibilities.

Strategic vision also plays a crucial role in this mindset shift. Rather than making isolated decisions about individual networking opportunities, I began developing a coherent investment strategy with clear goals and expected returns. This broader vision helped me evaluate each potential investment within a larger framework of relationship development rather than as disconnected expenses.

Perhaps most importantly, the access investment mindset requires a willingness to expand beyond comfortable, familiar environments. Many of the most valuable connection opportunities exist in settings that might initially feel uncomfortable or unfamiliar. The willingness to step into these spaces—not just physically but psychologically—opens doors to relationship possibilities that remaining in comfortable environments cannot provide.

The Premium Access Spectrum

Access investments exist along a spectrum from minimal to substantial, with different levels serving different strategic purposes. Understanding this spectrum helps you make more deliberate choices about where to invest your resources based on specific goals rather than merely pursuing the most exclusive options available.

The point isn't to break the bank for prestigious access or to be seen in exclusive circles, but rather to strategically invest in yourself by accessing different levels appropriate to your current situation. Weigh the potential benefits against costs, create a specific budget for access investments, and be able to clearly justify each expense based on the genuine opportunities it might create.

Remember that value often exists at various points along this spectrum—sometimes a mid-level industry conference might yield better returns for your specific goals than an ultra-premium gathering that strains your resources. Strategic positioning is about thoughtful allocation, not maximum spending.

My own access journey began with entry-level investments: professional organization memberships that cost a few hundred dollars annually and local networking events with modest registration fees. These initial positions created valuable connections within my immediate professional community and served as a foundation for understanding the basics of effective networking.

As my career progressed, I moved into mid-level access investments: industry conferences with higher registration costs, specialized training programs that created connections with peers and instructors, and professional development experiences that positioned me within more selective communities. These environments expanded my network beyond local connections while developing both capabilities and relationships simultaneously.

> **CONNECTION GEM:** *Different access levels serve different purposes. Strategic connectors invest at various points along this spectrum based on specific goals rather than simply pursuing the most exclusive options.*

Premium access investments followed as my career advanced further: executive education programs at leading business schools, exclusive industry gatherings with significant participation fees, and specialized conferences aimed at senior professionals. These environments created connections with higher-level decision-makers in more intimate settings than typical networking events could provide.

Ultra-premium access came next, including private mastermind groups with five-figure annual memberships and invitation-only retreats that combined learning, relationship building, and business development. These highly curated environments created deeper connections with carefully selected participants, generating opportunities for collaboration beyond what typical business relationships might offer.

Elite access—highly exclusive gatherings and private membership clubs—represents the highest level of this spectrum. While the investment required for these environments can be substantial, the relationship possibilities they create are often commensurate with their exclusivity. These settings provide access not just to individual connections but to entire networks that might otherwise remain inaccessible.

The key insight from understanding this spectrum is that different access levels serve different purposes. Rather than simply aspiring to the most exclusive options available, strategic connectors invest at various points along this spectrum based on specific goals, balancing accessibility with return potential.

Travel as Strategic Positioning

Some of my most valuable connections have emerged through strategic travel investments—deliberately choosing premium travel options that create unique networking opportunities. These investments go beyond mere comfort to create positioning that facilitates meaningful relationship development.

Premium travel—choosing business or first class rather than economy—represents more than just a comfortable seat. These premium cabins create natural conversation settings with fellow travelers who often include business leaders, investors, and other potential connection opportunities. The relaxed environment, extended time together, and natural conversation contexts facilitate relationship building in ways that forced networking rarely achieves.

This approach extends to airport lounges, which create pre-flight connection opportunities in comfortable, exclusive settings conducive to conversation. The investment in lounge access—whether through premium credit cards, airline status, or direct membership—positions you in environments where business travelers naturally congregate in more relaxed circumstances than typical airport settings provide.

> **CONNECTION GEM:** *Travel investments create both planned and serendipitous connection opportunities. The value often comes not just from intended meetings but from unexpected encounters that only premium positioning makes possible.*

About four years ago, I experienced a perfect example of this strategic positioning value. I was in New Orleans leaving Essence Fest in the Delta Sky Club lounge—a space you can't access without certain status on Delta and a specific premium credit card like the Platinum AmEx. While enjoying the quiet atmosphere away from the terminal chaos, I noticed Egypt Sherrod and Cynthia Bailey, both successful entrepreneurs and television personalities.

I noticed my friend Jamal was with them, and he said, "Nichole, come over; I want to introduce you to my friends Egypt and Cynthia." I engaged them in genuine conversation about their work and business interests. "What are you working on these days, and how might I be able to support you?" I asked. This value-first approach led to a meaningful exchange about their businesses and goals.

When we all returned to Atlanta, I organized a dinner to introduce them to my corporate network. I invited vice presidents from Fortune 500 companies alongside Egypt and Cynthia and also included my friend Yandy, who had relationships with both worlds. That initial dinner, born from a chance meeting made possible by strategic positioning in the Delta lounge, evolved into a quarterly gathering where each woman brings another successful female entrepreneur or high-profile executive.

What began as a single connection has grown into a powerful network of about twenty accomplished women who support each other's goals. We maintain an active group chat, share resources, and create opportunities for each other—all stemming from that initial meeting made possible by investing in lounge access. This network has become a cornerstone of my personal and professional life, demonstrating how access investments can yield returns far beyond their initial cost.

Strategic accommodation choices provide another dimension of travel-based positioning. Selecting hotels known for business travelers or industry gatherings creates additional connection opportunities beyond your primary travel purpose. The hotel bar, executive lounge, or breakfast area often facilitates casual conversations that can develop into valuable relationships.

Conference attendance, when strategically selected, represents another powerful travel investment. Rather than attending every event in your industry, focusing resources on the most valuable gatherings—those with the highest concentration of meaningful connection opportunities—creates more significant returns than dispersing your investment across too many events.

International positioning through global travel creates perhaps the broadest expansion of connection possibilities. Relationships developed across national boundaries often provide unique value through diverse perspectives, market access, and opportunity development that purely domestic networks cannot offer.

> **CONNECTION GEM:** *Premium environments often facilitate more natural, authentic connections than traditional networking settings. The investment creates not just proximity but favorable connection conditions.*

Membership-Based Access

Strategic membership investments create ongoing connection opportunities through sustained positioning in valuable environments. Unlike one-time events that provide limited interaction, memberships create continuing access that builds relationships over time through repeated exposure and shared community experience. I saw a networking need in my community and launched a Monthly Membership for my community to meet and grow their network and net worth.

Professional organizations represent the most common membership access investment. Industry-specific associations, professional societies, and trade groups provide ongoing connections to others in your field. While the explicit networking benefits are obvious, the implicit positioning value often comes through committee work, leadership roles, and other involvement that creates deeper relationships than merely attending events.

Business clubs offer more exclusive commercial networking environments with correspondingly higher investment requirements. These membership communities—whether traditional city clubs or modern coworking-based models—create ongoing access to accomplished professionals in comfortable settings designed for relationship building. The sustained nature of these environments allows relationships to develop naturally over time rather than forcing immediate connections.

> **CONNECTION GEM:** *Membership investments create sustained access rather than one-time opportunities. The cumulative value of ongoing presence often far exceeds the initial membership cost.*

Social clubs provide community-based connection settings that blend personal and professional relationship-building. While less explicitly business-focused than professional organizations or business clubs, these environments often facilitate deeper relationship development through shared interests beyond commercial concerns. These connections frequently evolve into valuable professional relationships precisely because they begin with a more personal foundation.

Charitable boards offer contribution-based leadership positioning that creates access to accomplished professionals while simultaneously serving community needs. Board service places you in regular contact with successful individuals in contexts that demonstrate your values and capabilities rather than just your networking interest. These environments create relationship depth through shared purpose and ongoing collaboration toward meaningful goals.

Alumni networks leverage educational affiliation into ongoing connection communities. Beyond simple association with institution names, active engagement with alumni organizations creates valuable relationship opportunities through shared experience and institutional loyalty. These connections often facilitate relationships across industry boundaries that might be difficult to develop through purely professional networking.

The power of membership-based access lies in its ongoing nature. Rather than the time-limited engagement of events or programs, memberships create sustained positioning that allows relationships to develop organically over extended periods. This cumulative effect often creates far greater value than the initial membership investment might suggest.

Digital Access Investments

Online environments also offer strategic positioning opportunities, sometimes with extraordinary return potential due to geographic boundary elimination. These digital investments create connection possibilities unconstrained by physical location, often at relatively low cost compared to in-person positioning.

CHAPTER 6: INVESTING IN ACCESS: STRATEGIC POSITIONING

Premium platform subscriptions provide enhanced networking capabilities on established digital services. Professional platforms like LinkedIn offer premium tiers that expand search, communication, and visibility features beyond basic access. These enhanced capabilities create connection opportunities that standard access doesn't provide, often at relatively modest investment levels.

Online community memberships position you within curated virtual connection spaces focused on specific industries or interests. These digital environments bring together professionals around shared concerns in structured settings that facilitate meaningful relationship building despite geographic distribution. The focused nature of these communities creates more valuable connections than general social platforms can provide.

> **CONNECTION GEM:** *Digital access investments often provide extraordinary ROI due to geographic boundary elimination. These investments can create global connection opportunities at relatively low cost compared to physical positioning.*

Digital course participation creates learning-based relationship opportunities similar to in-person educational investments but without geographic limitations. Beyond the explicit educational content, the relationship development with both instructors and fellow participants often creates lasting value that exceeds the knowledge gained. These connections frequently continue long after the formal course concludes.

Virtual mastermind groups provide exclusive online development communities that combine learning and relationship building in ongoing digital settings. These structured environments create deep connections through regular interaction and shared growth experiences despite participants' geographic distribution. The sustained nature of these groups builds relationship depth that is difficult to develop through isolated online events.

Content platform investments position you through digital visibility that creates passive connection opportunities. Whether through publishing platforms, video channels, or podcast networks, strategic content sharing establishes thought leadership that attracts valuable relationship opportunities without direct outreach. This approach creates connection possibilities that come to you rather than requiring active networking effort.

The extraordinary ROI potential of digital access investments comes from their geographic boundary elimination. These positioning strategies create connection opportunities with global reach at relatively low costs compared to physical positioning requiring travel and in-person presence. This leverage makes digital access particularly valuable for those building international networks or connecting across distributed industries.

The ROI of Access Investment

Understanding how to evaluate access investment returns helps optimize your strategic positioning approach. While traditional networking often produces difficult-to-measure results, thoughtful assessment frameworks can help evaluate whether specific investments are generating appropriate returns.

I learned this through systematically analyzing my own access investments over several years. By tracking both the costs of various positioning strategies and the relationship value they generated, I developed a clearer understanding of which approaches created the highest returns for my specific goals and circumstances.

Connection quality provides the most fundamental return measure—the caliber and relevance of relationships developed through specific positioning investments. Beyond simply counting connections, this assessment examines whether relationships align with your strategic objectives and create meaningful value exchange potential. A single high-value relationship often delivers a greater return than dozens of less relevant connections.

> **CONNECTION GEM:** *Access investment returns often materialize in unexpected ways and time frames. The most valuable opportunities frequently come not from anticipated connections but from serendipitous encounters that strategic positioning makes possible.*

Opportunity access represents another crucial return dimension—the doors opened through strategic positioning that wouldn't otherwise be available. These opportunities might include business possibilities, career advancement, resource access, or other valuable developments that positioning makes possible. Tracking these opportunity flows helps assess whether specific investments are creating meaningful returns.

Knowledge acquisition provides additional return beyond pure relationship development. Many access investments deliver valuable information and insights alongside connection opportunities. This knowledge value—whether industry intelligence, market trends, or specialized expertise—should be included when evaluating total investment return.

Visibility creation represents an often-overlooked return dimension—how strategic positioning enhances your professional visibility and reputation. Certain environments establish you within valuable networks in ways that create ongoing opportunity flows beyond specific relationships. This enhanced visibility often generates returns long after the initial positioning investment.

Long-term development—the cumulative benefits that accrue over extended periods—provides perhaps the most important return measure. Many access investments yield value that compounds over time rather than delivering immediate results. Evaluating these investments requires patience and a long-term perspective rather than expecting instant returns.

The most important insight about access investment ROI is that returns often materialize in unexpected ways and timeframes. The most valuable opportunities frequently come not from anticipated connections but from serendipitous encounters that strategic positioning makes possible. This unpredictability requires both patience and openness to recognize value that emerges in unanticipated forms.

Beyond Financial Investment

While this chapter focuses on strategic resource allocation, it's crucial to understand that access investment isn't solely financial. Many valuable positioning strategies require little or no monetary expenditure while still creating significant connection opportunities.

Time contribution through volunteering often creates powerful positioning without financial investment. Serving on event committees, helping coordinate industry gatherings, or supporting professional organizations places you in valuable settings while demonstrating commitment and capability. This involvement frequently creates deeper connections than merely attending events as a participant.

Expertise sharing represents another non-financial positioning strategy. By contributing knowledge through speaking, writing, or advising, you create value that positions you within premium environments without monetary investment. This contribution-based access often creates stronger relationships than paid positioning because it establishes you as a value provider rather than merely a participant.

> **CONNECTION GEM:** *For those with limited financial resources, non-monetary investments can create powerful access. Strategic contributions of time, expertise, and leadership often open doors that might otherwise require financial investment.*

Leadership service—taking on organizational responsibilities within professional communities—creates particularly valuable positioning through demonstrated capability rather than financial contribution. Committee leadership, special project management, or governance roles place you in close working relationships with accomplished professionals while showcasing your abilities in ways that create lasting impressions.

Content creation builds thought leadership positioning that attracts valuable connections rather than requiring you to pursue them. By sharing insights through articles, presentations, or digital media, you establish expertise that makes others seek relationships with you. This approach inverts traditional networking dynamics by creating inbound connection opportunities rather than requiring outbound effort.

Relationship development—building bridges that create access through existing connections—requires social rather than financial capital. By thoughtfully connecting people across networks, you create value that opens doors to new relationships and environments. This bridge-building positions you as a valuable connector whose access others seek to leverage.

CHAPTER 6: INVESTING IN ACCESS: STRATEGIC POSITIONING

These non-financial positioning strategies create particularly important opportunities for those early in their careers or with limited resources. By strategically investing time, expertise, and relationship capital, you can access environments that might otherwise seem financially inaccessible, creating connection opportunities despite resource constraints.

Navigating Exclusive Environments

Moving comfortably in premium environments requires understanding their cultural codes while maintaining authentic engagement. Each exclusive setting has unwritten rules that influence how relationships develop and interactions proceed. Understanding these norms while remaining genuine creates the most effective positioning. I firmly remind those who struggle with confidence or social anxiety: 'Own your presence—you have earned your place in every room you enter.'

This isn't empty encouragement but a fundamental truth about authentic positioning. Your unique perspective and value proposition belong in these spaces, regardless of how you arrived there. The most powerful presence comes not from mimicking others but from bringing your authentic self, enhanced by cultural understanding, into environments where your distinctive contribution can create the greatest impact.

> **CONNECTION GEM:** *Exclusive environments have their own cultural codes. Learning these unwritten rules while maintaining authenticity allows you to navigate premium settings effectively without compromising your values.*

Authentic engagement represents the crucial counterbalance to cultural adaptation—remaining genuine despite surroundings rather than adopting an artificial persona to fit exclusive settings. By bringing your true self to premium environments—while respecting their cultural norms—you create meaningful connections based on authentic relationships rather than superficial conformity.

Value contribution provides another essential navigation element—finding meaningful ways to add value within exclusive environments rather than simply receiving their benefits. By consistently looking for opportunities to help others, share useful insights, or make valuable introductions, you establish yourself as a community contributor rather than a mere participant, regardless of the setting's exclusivity.

Relationship building across status levels creates comprehensive connection value within premium environments. Rather than focusing exclusively on those with the highest apparent status, building genuine relationships throughout the community creates more diverse opportunity development and authentic engagement that transcends hierarchical limitations.

Purpose maintenance—staying focused on goals beyond the environment itself—prevents being seduced by exclusivity for its own sake. By maintaining clear objectives for your participation, you avoid the common trap of pursuing access as an end rather than as a means to meaningful relationship development aligned with substantive purpose.

These navigation approaches transform access from mere presence in exclusive settings to effective positioning that creates valuable connections. By understanding cultural context while maintaining authentic engagement, you develop relationships that create meaningful returns on your positioning investment rather than simply occupying premium space.

Creating Access for Others

True master connectors invest not just in their own access but in creating opportunities for others. This access creation represents perhaps the most powerful positioning approach—establishing yourself as someone who not only navigates exclusive environments but actively expands their accessibility to others with valuable contributions.

I began practicing this approach after recognizing how certain leaders had created transformative opportunities in my own journey by extending access they had established. Their generosity not only benefited those they helped but enhanced their own influence and relationship value by positioning them as connectors rather than merely networkers.

Introduction facilitation represents the most basic form of access creation—connecting people across barriers that might otherwise prevent their relationship development. By thoughtfully introducing individuals from different communities, you create value for both parties while establishing yourself as a valuable bridge between otherwise separate worlds.

> **CONNECTION GEM:** *Creating access for others generates extraordinary relationship value while establishing you as a generous connector rather than a self-interested networker.*

Mentorship provision helps others navigate exclusive environments that might otherwise prove challenging. By sharing insights about cultural norms, unwritten rules, and effective engagement approaches in premium settings, you help others succeed in environments where they might otherwise struggle despite gaining formal access.

Opportunity sharing extends access possibilities beyond your immediate use. By passing along invitations, membership openings, or participation chances you cannot personally utilize, you create value for others while establishing yourself as a generous connector focused on community benefit rather than personal advantage alone.

CHAPTER 6: INVESTING IN ACCESS: STRATEGIC POSITIONING

Advocacy development involves speaking up for talented individuals who might otherwise remain overlooked for valuable opportunities. By highlighting others' capabilities and potential contributions to selective environments, you create access they might not achieve independently while demonstrating a commitment to community enhancement rather than mere personal advancement.

System navigation support helps others understand the complex and often unstated rules governing exclusive environments. By making implicit expectations explicit for those new to premium settings, you create successful access where formal entry alone might prove insufficient for effective engagement and relationship development.

This access creation approach transforms your positioning from self-focused achievement to community-enhancing leadership. By investing in others' opportunities alongside your own, you establish a reputation as a generous connector whose relationship value extends far beyond a personal network to encompass broader access creation across communities and barriers.

Chapter Takeaways

1. Strategic positioning creates connection opportunities that effort alone cannot provide.
2. Access investments should be evaluated based on potential relationship return.

3. Different positioning environments serve different connection purposes.
4. Travel investments—from premium cabins to exclusive lounges—create unique networking opportunities worth considering strategically.
5. Non-financial investments can create powerful access for those with limited resources.
6. Authentic engagement remains essential regardless of positioning level.
7. Creating access for others builds extraordinary relationship capital.
8. Thoughtful strategy significantly enhances positioning return on investment.

Action Steps

1. **Conduct an Access Investment Audit**
   - ☐ Evaluate current positioning environments.
   - ☐ Assess the return on existing investments.
   - ☐ Identify gaps in strategic positioning.
   - ☐ Analyze highest-value opportunities.
   - ☐ Consider access barriers to target relationships.
2. **Develop Your Investment Strategy**
   - ☐ Clarify specific positioning goals.
   - ☐ Identify primary access targets.
   - ☐ Create a resource allocation approach.

- ☐ Build a progressive investment timeline.
- ☐ Establish return evaluation metrics.

3. **Build Your Access Value Proposition**
   - ☐ Define your unique contributions.
   - ☐ Develop environment-specific approaches.
   - ☐ Create your positioning narrative.
   - ☐ Establish authentic engagement strategies.
   - ☐ Plan value delivery in target environments.

4. **Create Your Navigation Approach**
   - ☐ Research environment-specific cultural codes.
   - ☐ Develop authentic adaptation strategies.
   - ☐ Build relationship development approaches.
   - ☐ Create cross-environment connection plans.
   - ☐ Establish comfort expansion practices.

5. **Establish Your Ethical Framework**
   - ☐ Define personal positioning boundaries.
   - ☐ Create value contribution commitments.
   - ☐ Develop access-sharing approaches.
   - ☐ Build authentic engagement practices.
   - ☐ Establish purpose alignment principle.

As you develop your strategic positioning approach, remember that access investment represents one of the most underappreciated aspects of high-level networking. While relationship skills remain fundamental, deliberately placing yourself in environments where valuable connections naturally occur dramatically increases your opportunities.

In the next chapter, we'll explore how to leverage business resource groups to build powerful connections within organizations.

> **Final Connection Gem:** *Most people wait for opportunities. Strategic connectors position themselves for them. In a world where access is often uneven, your ability to remove barriers—not just for yourself but for others—will set you apart. Because access isn't given. It's created. When approached ethically and authentically, access investment becomes not just a personal advancement tool but a means of creating more equitable opportunity distribution through thoughtful relationship building.*

CHAPTER 7

Business Resource Groups as Connection Accelerators

"Some of the most powerful professional connections come not from external networking events, but from strategically engaging with groups right within your organization."

The first time I stepped onto the trading floor on Wall Street, I felt like an outsider. I was a young Black woman from an HBCU, surrounded by Ivy League graduates who seemed to speak in a coded language I hadn't been taught. The room hummed with conversations, but none of them included me.

I knew that relationships were the key to survival in this high-stakes environment—but how could I build them when I didn't even know where to start?

The answer came from an unexpected place: Business Resource Groups (BRGs).

The answer came in an unexpected form: Business Resource Groups (BRGs), also sometimes called Employee Resource Groups (ERGs). These internal communities, originally created to support diversity and inclusion initiatives, became my secret weapon for building powerful connections throughout the organization. Not only did I join the groups aligned with my own identity as a Black woman, but I also strategically engaged with groups representing completely different communities—veterans, LGBTQ+ employees, Asian, Hispanic, and more.

This approach transformed my networking possibilities. Instead of being limited to connections on my immediate team, I gained access to relationships throughout the organization—across departments, hierarchical levels, and functional areas. These connections accelerated my career growth, provided crucial support during challenges, and eventually helped me build bridges between the corporate and entrepreneurial worlds.

In this chapter, I'll share how you can leverage BRGs as powerful connection engines, whether you're navigating a corporate environment or engaging with these groups as an external partner.

CHAPTER 7: BUSINESS RESOURCE GROUPS AS CONNECTION ACCELERATORS

Understanding Business Resource Groups

The first time I heard about Business Resource Groups was during my corporate orientation. The HR representative briefly mentioned them among various employee programs, but I didn't grasp their significance until weeks later when a colleague invited me to attend a Black Professionals Network meeting.

Walking into that first gathering, I was struck by the diversity within this group that shared my racial identity. There were people from every department of the organization—finance professionals, marketing specialists, technology experts, operations managers—spanning from entry-level positions to senior executives. In that moment, I realized these groups weren't just social clubs but potential networks cutting across the organizational chart in ways that normal work relationships rarely did.

Business Resource Groups, or Employee Resource Groups, are voluntary, employee-led communities within organizations that share common characteristics, experiences, or interests. While they often begin with identity-focused groups around race, gender, or sexual orientation, they frequently expand to include interest-based communities like parents, environmental advocates, or wellness enthusiasts.

During my first year, I discovered the rich variety of these groups within my organization. Beyond the cultural and ethnic groups like Black, Hispanic/Latino, and Asian networks, there were gender-based communities like women's networks and working mother groups. The LGBTQ+ employees and allies had a particularly active presence, as did military veterans. There were groups for employees with disabilities, generational communities like young professionals, and interest-based networks around wellness, sustainability, and community service.

> **CONNECTION GEM:** *Even in organizations without formal BRG structures, informal communities often exist that serve similar functions. Look for these natural groupings and engage strategically.*

What surprised me about these groups was their evolution over time. A senior colleague explained how BRGs had transformed from their origins. "Fifteen years ago, BRGs were mainly support groups—safe spaces for underrepresented employees to connect. Today, they're business accelerators.

Take the Women's Network at my firm, for example. What started as a casual lunch gathering for female employees is now a corporate-backed initiative shaping company policy, advising on consumer trends, and developing future executives.

BRGs aren't just about belonging anymore—they're about power. And if you learn how to leverage them, they can be game-changers for your career."

This evolution became clear as I observed the diverse functions these groups served. While they still provided valuable support and community, they also offered professional development programming, created marketplace insights about diverse consumers, and served as innovation incubators for the company. Many of the senior executives I met had built their leadership capabilities through BRG involvement earlier in their careers.

> **CONNECTION GEM:** *Understanding this evolution helps you engage with BRGs at their highest value level. While support remains important, the strategic business impact of these groups creates their most powerful connection opportunities.*

BRGs as Connection Accelerators

In my third month at the firm, I attended a panel discussion hosted by the Women's Network. Afterward, during the informal networking reception, I struck up a conversation with Jessica, a senior executive from a department I had never interacted with professionally. When I mentioned a challenge my team was facing with a particular trading platform, she immediately connected me with someone in her division who had solved a similar problem.

This kind of cross-functional connection simply wouldn't have happened in the normal course of my work. My daily interactions were primarily limited to my immediate team and occasionally to other groups in the same division. The BRG created a bridge across organizational boundaries that wouldn't otherwise exist.

As I became more involved in various groups, I discovered the unique networking advantages they offered. They provided access to relationships across departmental boundaries, creating connections I couldn't have made through my normal work channels. They built bridges across hierarchical levels, allowing me to develop relationships with both senior leaders and promising junior employees throughout the organization. Perhaps most importantly, these connections formed around shared purpose and interests rather than just work functions, creating stronger bonds than typical workplace relationships.

> **CONNECTION GEM:** *BRGs allow you to build relationships outside your immediate team or department, creating a network web throughout the organization rather than just within your functional silo.*

The structural support these groups received from the organization added another dimension to their networking value. Unlike informal gatherings or ad hoc connections, BRGs had organizational backing—budget, leadership support, and official recognition. This institutional sanction created legitimacy that enhanced relationship development within their frameworks.

I also discovered how these groups provided unique access to senior leadership. Many BRGs had executive sponsors who regularly attended events and took a genuine interest in members' development. These touchpoints created visibility with organizational leaders I would rarely encounter in my normal role. I encourage you to not only join these BRG groups, but to take a leadership role in them, which will help you stand out to senior leaders who are involved.

My BRG Strategy: Beyond Identity Groups

While many employees joined only the groups aligned with their personal identities, I developed a different approach. After actively participating in the Black employee network and women's group for several months, I noticed an announcement for a Veterans BRG event featuring a panel on leadership lessons from military experience. Though I had no military background myself, the topic intrigued me, and I decided to attend.

Walking into that event, I immediately felt like an outsider. The room was filled primarily with veterans sharing experiences I couldn't relate to directly. But rather than retreating, I approached the experience with genuine curiosity. During the discussion period, I asked thoughtful questions about how military leadership principles might apply in our corporate environment.

After the event, several veteran members approached me, appreciative of my interest in their experiences. One of them, Marcus, was particularly welcoming. "Most non-veterans never come to these events," he said. "They assume they don't belong or wouldn't get value from the discussions. Your questions showed real interest in understanding our perspective."

> **CONNECTION GEM:** *Engaging with groups beyond your own identity demonstrates genuine interest in diverse perspectives and creates relationship opportunities that same-group networking cannot provide.*

This initial positive experience led me to explore other groups where I didn't share the core identity. I attended LGBTQ+ ally events, participated in programs hosted by the parents' network despite not having children, and joined sustainability initiatives through the environmental group. Each of these cross-identity engagements created unique connections that wouldn't have formed if I had limited myself to only "my" groups.

As my involvement deepened, I took on responsibilities in selected groups—coordinating a mentoring program for the Black professionals' network and helping organize a leadership development workshop for the women's group. These leadership roles enhanced my visibility and demonstrated capabilities that might not be apparent in my day-to-day work.

Perhaps most valuably, I began building bridges between different BRGs. When I noticed that both the Black professionals and veterans groups were planning similar career development programs, I suggested combining resources for a joint event that would benefit both communities while promoting cross-group connections.

Throughout all these engagements, I maintained a consistent focus on adding value. Rather than approaching BRGs as networking opportunities to be exploited, I looked for ways to contribute meaningfully to each group's success—offering marketing expertise for event promotion, connecting groups with potential speakers, or sharing relevant resources. This value-first approach made my cross-group participation welcome rather than intrusive.

BRGs as Leadership Development Platforms

Six months into my BRG involvement, I noticed something interesting about these groups' leadership structures. Many of the people taking on significant leadership roles within BRGs were performing at levels seemingly beyond their official positions in the organization. A junior marketing coordinator was masterfully leading the Hispanic network's strategic planning process. An administrative assistant was skillfully managing the complex budget for the LGBTQ+ group's annual conference.

"BRGs are leadership laboratories," explained Diane, a mentor who had risen to senior management partly through her own BRG involvement years earlier. "They give people chances to develop and demonstrate capabilities that might be constrained in their formal roles."

As I took on more responsibility within several groups, I experienced this leadership development dimension firsthand.

Coordinating the Black professionals' mentoring initiative provided an opportunity to demonstrate project management skills beyond those required in my trading role. Leading the marketing committee for a women's leadership conference showcased strategic thinking and execution capabilities that weren't visible in my day-to-day work.

> **CONNECTION GEM:** *BRG leadership roles allow you to demonstrate capabilities to decision-makers who might not otherwise see your potential. These groups often function as leadership proving grounds that create advancement opportunities.*

These roles created valuable visibility with decision-makers throughout the organization. When I presented the mentoring program results to our executive committee, several senior leaders saw capabilities they wouldn't have observed through my normal reporting structure. This visibility later led to inquiries about my interest in emerging leadership opportunities.

The executive exposure through BRG involvement proved particularly valuable. Working with senior sponsors and advisors created relationships that would have been difficult to establish otherwise. When the global diversity officer attended our planning meeting and was impressed by my approach to measuring program effectiveness, it created a connection that later opened doors to broader organizational initiatives.

Cross-functional leadership experience through BRG initiatives developed capabilities beyond those available in my specialized trading role. Managing projects across departments built collaborative skills and a broader organizational understanding that enhanced my overall professional development.

Perhaps most importantly, BRG leadership created natural skill development in organization, communication, and influence—capabilities essential for advancement but sometimes difficult to build in entry-level positions. Learning to motivate volunteers, manage without formal authority, and navigate organizational politics through these roles accelerated my leadership growth beyond what my official position alone could have provided.

BRGs and Executive Sponsorship

One of the most valuable aspects of BRG involvement proved to be the executive sponsorship dimension. Each group had senior leaders who served as sponsors, providing organizational support, strategic guidance, and often personal mentorship to group members.

I discovered this value through my work with the women's leadership committee, which was sponsored by Patricia, the Chief Operating Officer. Initially, I was intimidated by her senior position and limited my interactions to formal group settings. Then, during a planning session for an upcoming conference, I offered a suggestion about measuring the event's impact that caught Patricia's attention.

"That's an interesting approach," she said. "Could you elaborate on how you'd implement that measurement framework?"

What followed was a fifteen-minute discussion where I outlined the assessment methodology I envisioned. Patricia asked thoughtful questions that helped refine the approach, and by the end of the conversation, she had asked me to lead the impact measurement workstream for the conference.

> **CONNECTION GEM:** *BRG executive sponsors often become champions for talented members they identify through group activities. These relationships can create career opportunities far beyond your immediate work environment.*

This interaction taught me the value of understanding the executive sponsorship dimension of BRGs. I began researching which leaders supported which groups and what specific aspects of the groups' work particularly interested them. This knowledge helped me identify potential connection opportunities aligned with both my capabilities and their priorities.

I also learned the importance of demonstrating value through group contributions. Rather than attempting to build relationships with sponsors directly, I focused on making meaningful contributions to group initiatives they cared about. This authentic engagement naturally created opportunities for interaction that felt purposeful rather than forced.

Appropriate engagement proved essential in developing these relationships. I approached sponsor interactions with respect for their position while demonstrating capability through my work. This balanced approach—neither overly familiar nor unnecessarily deferential—created productive professional relationships.

Problem-solving focus particularly resonated with executive sponsors. When I helped address a challenge with the Black professionals' mentoring program metrics that the CHRO had specifically requested, it created visibility with him that would have been difficult to achieve through my normal role.

I also learned the importance of visibility balance—demonstrating value without inappropriate self-promotion. By focusing on group success rather than personal recognition, I ironically gained more positive attention from sponsors than those overtly seeking it. This authentic approach to sponsor relationships created advocate relationships that significantly enhanced my organizational influence.

BRGs and Career Mobility

Perhaps the most significant personal benefit of my BRG involvement emerged through its impact on my career mobility. Two years in, an opportunity came up that felt completely out of reach—a role in our strategic initiatives group. It was several levels above my current position, and I didn't have the "right" credentials. I almost didn't apply.

But then I remembered something.

Through my BRG leadership, I had led cross-functional projects, worked directly with senior executives, and solved complex business challenges.

I didn't just have experience—I had proven impact.

So, I applied.

When I got the interview, I was stunned. But what shocked me even more was what the hiring manager said.

During the interview, the hiring manager referenced specific capabilities she had observed through my BRG leadership. "I was impressed by how you managed the cross-group financial empowerment program," she said. "It demonstrated leadership, strategy, and execution—exactly what we need in this role."

That's when it hit me: My BRG work had made me more visible than my actual job ever did. The leadership roles, project management experience, and organizational impact I'd demonstrated through these groups had effectively expanded my qualified opportunity range beyond what my official title and tenure would suggest.

CHAPTER 7: BUSINESS RESOURCE GROUPS AS CONNECTION ACCELERATORS

> **CONNECTION GEM:** *BRGs often function as unofficial leadership development programs. The capabilities and relationships built through these groups create advancement opportunities that might otherwise be inaccessible.*

Mentor access provided another crucial career mobility advantage. Through BRG involvement, I had developed relationships with experienced guides across different organizational functions who provided valuable coaching during my interview preparation. These mentors offered perspective on the hiring department's priorities and helped me position my experience effectively—advantages I wouldn't have had through my normal work relationships alone.

Development opportunities through BRG-sponsored training and growth resources had enhanced my qualifications for advancement. Workshops on strategic communication, leadership development programs, and project management training made available through these groups had built capabilities relevant to my target role without requiring formal educational investment.

Reputation building through positive visibility organization-wide had perhaps the greatest impact on my career mobility. Rather than being known only within my immediate department, I had established a positive reputation across multiple functions through BRG contributions. This broader recognition created advocates for my advancement beyond my direct management chain.

Most importantly, BRG involvement had provided leadership preparation that developed capabilities for higher-level roles before I formally held them. By managing complex initiatives, guiding diverse teams, and navigating organizational dynamics through these groups, I had essentially been practicing the skills required for advancement before officially moving into positions that required them.

When I ultimately received the strategic initiatives role, skipping two traditional career steps in the process, I recognized how powerfully BRG involvement had accelerated my career mobility. These groups had functioned as unofficial leadership development programs that created advancement opportunities that might otherwise have been inaccessible based solely on my formal position.

BRGs and Personal Brand Development

About two years into my BRG involvement, I noticed something interesting. People who had never worked directly with me often approached me at company events with comments like, "You're the one who organized that amazing financial education program," or "I heard about your work with the community recruitment initiative." Without deliberately planning it, my BRG contributions had significantly shaped my professional reputation throughout the organization.

This observation helped me recognize how strategic group involvement could enhance personal brand development in ways that normal job performance alone might not achieve. My regular role as a trader provided limited visibility across the organization, but my BRG leadership had created broader recognition for specific capabilities and contributions.

Through reflection on this unplanned brand development, I began more deliberately leveraging BRG involvement for expertise showcase. By leading initiatives aligned with my professional strengths and interests—marketing for the women's leadership conference, analytics for the mentoring program assessment—I established recognition for these capabilities beyond my immediate team.

> **CONNECTION GEM:** *BRGs provide platforms for demonstrating your unique value proposition to a broader audience than your immediate team. This visibility helps establish your personal brand across the organization.*

Value consistency through reliable BRG contributions significantly enhanced my professional reputation. By consistently delivering on commitments—meeting deadlines, producing quality work, and following through on promises—I established a reputation for reliability that transferred to perceptions of my overall professional capability. This consistency created trust that enhanced my organizational credibility beyond specific group contributions.

Visibility creation through BRG leadership positioned me as someone with capabilities beyond my official role and level.

When I presented our cross-group initiative results to the executive committee, it created exposure to senior leadership that my trading position would not have provided for years. This visibility accelerated recognition of my potential for advancement beyond standard career progression timelines.

My BRG involvement also contributed to story development around my professional narrative. The projects I led, the challenges I addressed, and the impacts I created through these groups became part of how people understood my capabilities and potential. These stories—"Remember how she managed that complex event with half the expected budget?"—became reference points that enhanced my professional reputation in ways my regular responsibilities alone might not have generated.

These relationship reinforcements through broad connection development across the organization created widespread advocates for my advancement. Rather than depending solely on my direct manager's assessment, I had supporters throughout the company who had directly experienced my capabilities through BRG collaboration. This distributed advocacy significantly enhanced my promotion potential compared to colleagues with similar technical skills but more limited organizational visibility.

This personal brand development dimension transformed how I viewed BRG involvement—not just as a community contribution or networking opportunity, but as a strategic platform for establishing my professional reputation and value proposition throughout the organization. By thoughtfully aligning my group contributions with the professional identity I hoped to establish, I created brand development that significantly enhanced my career advancement potential.

BRGs as External Relationship Channels

While BRGs primarily serve internal networking functions, I discovered they also provide unique pathways for external relationships. As the leader of the Black professionals' community engagement committee, I built connections with community organizations, educational institutions, and other companies' affinity groups that created valuable relationships beyond our organization.

The external liaison function of many BRGs naturally creates meeting opportunities with professionals from other companies and institutions. When coordinating a joint volunteer event with other financial firms' diversity groups, I connected with counterparts throughout the industry. These relationships provided valuable perspectives, competitive intelligence, and potential career opportunities that expanded my network far beyond internal connections alone.

> **CONNECTION GEM:** *BRGs often create external networking opportunities that might not be available through standard professional roles. These external connections can provide particularly valuable perspectives and career development relationships.*

The industry landscape dimension of BRG cross-company engagement created especially useful context. By interacting with diverse professionals across multiple organizations, I developed a broader understanding of industry trends, competitive practices, and career paths than my specific role would have provided. This expanded perspective significantly enhanced my strategic thinking and career planning.

Vendor and supplier connections facilitated through BRG initiatives created additional relationship value. When organizing the women's leadership conference, I worked with various event partners, speakers, and service providers who became valuable additions to my professional network. These connections with external professionals often yielded insights and opportunities beyond our specific project engagements.

Charitable and community organization partnerships fostered through BRG outreach provided particularly meaningful external connections. When leading volunteer initiatives with nonprofit groups, I built relationships with community leaders, program directors, and other professionals from diverse backgrounds.

These external connections enriched my perspective while creating potential future partnerships.

Board and governance opportunities sometimes emerged from these external BRG connections as well. My effective coordination of cross-organizational networking events led to an invitation to join a nonprofit advisory board that further expanded my professional network and leadership experience.

These external relationship benefits complemented the internal networking value of BRGs, creating comprehensive connection development both within and beyond my organization. By leveraging BRG involvement for both internal and external relationship building, I created a more diverse, resilient professional network than either dimension alone could have provided.

Chapter Takeaways

1. BRGs provide unique networking opportunities across organizational boundaries.
2. Strategic engagement beyond identity groups creates distinctive connection value.
3. Group leadership roles offer visibility to decision-makers throughout the organization.
4. Bridge-building between different BRGs positions you as a valuable connector.

5. BRGs increasingly serve as pipelines to leadership and external relationship channels.
6. Executive sponsorship through BRGs can create career-changing advocacy.
7. BRG involvement shapes your personal brand and professional reputation.

Action Steps

1. **Conduct a BRG Landscape Analysis**
   - ☐ Identify available groups in your organization.
   - ☐ Research their focus and activities.
   - ☐ Understand leadership and sponsorship structures.
   - ☐ Assess connection opportunities in each group.
   - ☐ Evaluate which groups align with your goals.
2. **Develop Your Engagement Strategy**
   - ☐ Select primary and secondary involvement targets.
   - ☐ Identify specific value you can contribute.
   - ☐ Create a balanced participation approach.
   - ☐ Map key relationship opportunities.
   - ☐ Establish engagement boundaries.

3. **Build Your BRG Value Proposition**
   - ☐ Define your unique contributions.
   - ☐ Develop specific skills to showcase.
   - ☐ Create your group engagement narrative.
   - ☐ Establish connection objectives.
   - ☐ Plan your leadership development path.

4. **Create Your Bridge-Building Approach**
   - ☐ Identify connection opportunities between groups.
   - ☐ Develop cross-BRG initiative ideas.
   - ☐ Build relationships with multiple group leaders.
   - ☐ Create value across community boundaries.
   - ☐ Establish yourself as a connector.

5. **Establish Your Measurement Approach**
   - ☐ Define success metrics for your engagement.
   - ☐ Create tracking mechanisms for relationships.
   - ☐ Establish regular assessment practices.
   - ☐ Set connection development milestones.
   - ☐ Plan strategy adjustments based on outcomes.

As you develop your BRG engagement strategy, remember that these groups represent one of the most underutilized networking resources in most organizations. While many professionals view them primarily as diversity initiatives or social communities, strategic connectors recognize their power as relationship accelerators and leadership development platforms.

In the next chapter, we'll explore how to build your personal brand through relationships, creating a reputation that naturally attracts opportunities through authentic connection rather than self-promotion.

> **Final Connection Gem:** *In the corporate world, titles separate people. Departments divide them. But BRGs? They build bridges. They give you access, visibility, and influence—if you use them wisely. Most people see them as social groups. The Master Connector sees them as accelerators. The question isn't whether you should join one. The question is: How will you use them to build the career and connections you want?*

CHAPTER 8

Building Your Personal Brand Through Relationships

"Your personal brand isn't what you say about yourself—it's what other people say about you when you're not in the room."

"We need someone like Nichole Harmon-Pointdujour for this." The executive's voice cut through the meeting room chatter. "She's known for bringing people together across industries and making things happen." Another nodded. "Everything she touches seems to work. Her events always have the right people in the room."

I sat there, taking it in. Not just the words, but what they meant. My name had become synonymous with connection, execution, and results—not because I had marketed myself that way, but because of the relationships I had built over time. Without any deliberate "branding strategy," my reputation was working for me, even when I wasn't in the room.

And that's when I realized: The most powerful personal brand isn't crafted. It's experienced.

This experience highlights a crucial truth about effective personal branding: while traditional approaches focus on self-presentation through carefully crafted messages and curated social media, the most powerful personal brands emerge through consistent relationship experiences. What people say about you when you're not in the room ultimately matters far more than what you say about yourself.

In this chapter, we'll explore the relationship-centered approach to personal branding—how to build a reputation that naturally attracts opportunities through authentic connection rather than calculated self-promotion.

Understanding Relationship-Based Personal Branding

Early in my career, I was fascinated by personal branding books that focused on crafting perfect elevator pitches, designing beautiful business cards, and curating social media profiles. I diligently followed their advice, creating what I thought was a compelling personal brand through careful messaging. Yet, for all this effort, few opportunities emerged from these deliberate branding activities.

Meanwhile, almost accidentally, I was building something much more powerful through my daily work habits and relationship patterns. My consistent follow-through on commitments, fast execution style on deliverables, thoughtful connection-making, and genuine interest in others' success began creating a reputation that opened doors without my direct effort.

This experience made me rethink everything I had been taught about personal branding. The biggest difference? Traditional branding tells people what to believe about you. Relationship branding shows them.

Traditional Branding includes:	Relationship-Based Branding includes:
Focuses on self-presentation	Focuses on creating value for others
Relies on a curated online presence	Built through real interactions & trust
Messaging-driven (what you say about yourself)	Experience-driven (what others say about you)
Seeks visibility first	Seeks impact first
About "who you claim to be"	About "what people actually experience with you"

> **CONNECTION GEM:** *The most powerful personal brands aren't consciously created—they're the natural byproduct of consistent, authentic interaction patterns. Focus on creating value in relationships, and a powerful brand naturally emerges. People will always remember how you treated them; I always treat everyone with the same level of respect, no matter their title.*

Conventional branding emphasizes image management, while relationship branding develops through behavioral consistency. The traditional approach focuses on personal promotion; relationship branding emerges from the value you consistently contribute to others. Perhaps most importantly, traditional branding involves the strategic crafting of a public image, while relationship-based reputation develops organically through authentic interactions.

This understanding transformed my approach to professional reputation development. Rather than focusing on how to present myself, I began concentrating on what experience people had when interacting with me. This subtle shift created more authentic and effective results than deliberate personal branding efforts ever had.

The Relationship Brand Mindset

My perspective on personal branding fundamentally changed during a conversation with Christina, a highly successful executive who seemed to attract opportunities without obvious self-promotion. When I asked about her personal branding strategy, she looked puzzled.

"I don't think about branding myself," she explained. "I focus on creating consistent value for the people I work with. The reputation takes care of itself."

This deceptively simple approach contained profound wisdom that revealed the essential mindset for relationship-based branding. Rather than asking "How do I want to be perceived?" Christina focused on "What experience do I want people to have when they interact with me?" This subtle reframing completely changes the approach to personal reputation building.

> **CONNECTION GEM:** *Shift from asking "How do I want to be perceived?" to "What experience do I want people to have when they interact with me?" This subtle change creates more authentic and effective personal branding.*

The relationship brand mindset begins with service orientation—focusing primarily on creating value for others rather than promoting yourself. It requires authentic consistency, being reliably yourself across different contexts rather than adapting a persona for different audiences. Impact awareness—understanding how your actions affect others' experiences—becomes more important than crafting perfect messages.

Reputation consciousness means recognizing that every interaction shapes your brand, not just deliberately crafted communications. A long-term perspective builds brand equity through sustained patterns rather than quick impression management. This mindset creates a foundation for authentic reputation development that emerges naturally from genuine relationship habits rather than calculated brand management.

Identifying Your Relationship Brand Elements

While relationship branding emerges organically, awareness of your distinctive qualities can enhance its effectiveness. I discovered this when seeking feedback from trusted colleagues about their experience working with me. Their responses revealed patterns I hadn't consciously recognized but that consistently shaped others' experiences with me.

They mentioned my reliability in following through on commitments, my ability to connect with different types of people, my skill at making complex concepts understandable, and my talent for creating comfortable environments where meaningful conversation could happen. These weren't qualities I had deliberately crafted as brand elements, but they consistently characterized the experience people had when interacting with me.

CHAPTER 8: BUILDING YOUR PERSONAL BRAND THROUGH RELATIONSHIPS

> **CONNECTION GEM:** *Understanding your natural relationship patterns helps you lean into authentic strengths rather than trying to fabricate qualities that don't naturally exist. True relationship branding amplifies genuine attributes rather than manufacturing false ones.*

This feedback helped me identify my natural strengths—inherent capabilities that came easily rather than skills I had to force. It revealed my consistent behaviors—reliable patterns in how I operated that others had come to expect. I saw clear value patterns in how I typically contributed to others' success and characteristic relationship approaches that defined my interaction style.

Most importantly, I recognized impact areas where I consistently created positive results—particular types of problems I naturally solved effectively. Understanding these elements allowed me to lean into authentic strengths rather than trying to create an artificial professional persona that didn't align with my genuine qualities.

This self-awareness doesn't involve inventing brand elements but rather recognizing patterns that already exist in your relationships. The goal isn't to manufacture qualities but to understand and intentionally amplify your authentic strengths in ways that create consistent value for others.

Case Study: The Evolution of My Relationship Brand

My own personal brand has evolved through several distinct phases, each built primarily through relationship experiences rather than deliberate branding efforts. This evolution happened naturally as my capabilities and focus areas developed over time, creating different but connected reputation elements.

Early in my career, I unknowingly built my first personal brand: "The Reliable Performer."

I remember one night when a major deadline was suddenly moved up. My team panicked, unsure how we'd meet it. But I stayed up, powered through, and had the report on my manager's desk before dawn.

The next morning, she glanced at it, nodded, and said, "I don't even need to check it—I know it's right."

That moment taught me something powerful: Being reliable isn't just a work ethic; it's a brand.

People started to associate my name with trust, execution, and results. That's how personal branding works—not through words, but through experience. The key was consistency in meeting commitments, not deliberate brand messaging.

As my career progressed, I developed recognition as "the bridge-builder"—someone who could connect different worlds and perspectives to create value. This reputation emerged from regularly bringing together people from different departments, industries, and backgrounds who wouldn't otherwise connect. The consistent pattern of facilitating these connections, not self-promotion, created this reputation element.

> **CONNECTION GEM:** *Authentic personal brands evolve organically through career phases rather than being static creations. Allow your relationship brand to develop naturally as your capabilities and contributions grow.*

Later, I became known as "the value creator"—someone who could generate results across different contexts and challenges. This reputation grew from consistently finding ways to solve problems and create positive outcomes in various situations. Again, the actual results, not claims about my capabilities, built this reputation element.

Eventually, I established recognition as "the master connector"—someone known specifically for bringing together valuable relationships in strategic ways to help generate profits. This culminated in my reputation as "the experience curator"—creating distinctive environments for meaningful connection between diverse participants.

Throughout this evolution, my focus remained on creating consistent experiences rather than promoting a particular image. The reputation emerged from patterns of behavior rather than calculated brand messaging, evolving naturally as my capabilities and contributions grew.

The Relationship Consistency Principle

Consistent experience across interactions forms the foundation of powerful relationship brands. I learned this principle through both positive and negative examples throughout my career. Those with the strongest professional reputations weren't necessarily the most talented but were the most reliable in creating consistent positive experiences.

I observed this with my colleague Constance, who wasn't always the most innovative thinker but developed an extraordinary reputation through absolute reliability. Whether in small commitments like arriving on time for meetings or major promises like project deliverables, she created a consistent experience of dependability that became her defining professional characteristic.

This consistency appeared in multiple dimensions. Her value delivery reliably created benefits for others rather than just meeting minimum requirements. Her follow-through meant consistently doing what she said she would do, creating trust through reliability. Her behavioral patterns maintained recognizable interaction approaches that others could anticipate and count on.

> **CONNECTION GEM:** *Consistency creates trust, which forms the foundation of a powerful relationship brand. When people can reliably predict the experience of working with you, your personal brand strengthens automatically. You want to be known as the person who executes with excellence.*

Constance maintained consistent quality standards, upholding reliable performance levels rather than dramatic fluctuations between excellence and mediocrity. Perhaps most importantly, she demonstrated unwavering core values—principles that remained consistent regardless of circumstances.

This consistency principle explains why relationship brands can't be fabricated quickly. They require sustained patterns of behavior that others experience repeatedly, creating a reliable foundation for reputation development. When people can predict with confidence what the experience of working with you will be like, your personal brand strengthens automatically through this consistency rather than through deliberate promotion.

Digital Relationship Branding

Online environments require specific approaches to relationship-based branding. I discovered this when my carefully curated social media presence failed to generate meaningful professional opportunities despite substantial follower counts and engagement metrics. Meanwhile, a more authentic approach focused on consistent value sharing created significant relationship development.

The turning point came when I stopped trying to "curate" my brand online and started focusing on three things:

The "Give-Engage-Show" Framework for Digital Branding:

- Give → Share valuable insights, tools, or resources. Instead of just posting a quote, offer real strategies that help others.
- Engage → Don't just "like" posts—start conversations. Ask insightful questions. Add thoughtful comments.
- Show → Demonstrate your expertise through action. Instead of announcing your achievements, highlight team wins, collaborations, and shared lessons.

Once I shifted to this approach, my online presence stopped feeling like self-promotion—and started feeling like a magnet for real connections. This consistent value sharing established a reputation for contribution rather than self-promotion.

Authentic engagement—responding thoughtfully to others' content and questions rather than using automated or superficial responses—created meaningful relationship development despite digital distance. Cross-platform alignment maintained a consistent presence across different channels, avoiding the fragmented identity that undermines relationship trust.

> **CONNECTION GEM:** *Digital environments should extend your in-person relationship brand rather than creating a disconnected online persona. Focus on providing the same quality of experience online that people would have with you in person. Providing value-added information online helps increase engagement.*

Community building—creating meaningful connections between people in my network, not just with me—enhanced my reputation as a connector rather than just a content creator. Value-focused content sharing demonstrated expertise through genuinely helpful information rather than claims about my capabilities.

The most important insight was that digital environments should extend your in-person relationship brand rather than create a disconnected online persona. By focusing on providing the same quality of experience online that people would have with me in person, my digital presence strengthened rather than contradicted my overall professional reputation.

Reputation Acceleration Through Strategic Relationships

Certain connections can significantly accelerate relationship-based brand development. I experienced this when Justin, a highly respected industry leader, began mentioning my work in his presentations and introducing me to his extensive network. His endorsement created opportunities and recognition that would have taken years to develop independently.

This experience revealed the power of strategic relationships in reputation development. Justin functioned as a credibility partner—a high-reputation individual whose association enhanced others' perception of my work. His vocal advocacy actively promoted my capabilities to audiences I couldn't have reached directly. As an opportunity provider, he created chances to demonstrate my value in settings that would otherwise have been inaccessible.

> **CONNECTION GEM:** *While maintaining an authentic relationship focus, strategically develop connections with those who can amplify your reputation. These accelerator relationships create compound returns on your relationship investments.*

Other accelerator relationships came through feedback contributors—individuals who helped refine my effectiveness through honest assessment and guidance. Visibility enhancers increased my exposure to new audiences through their platforms and networks, creating broader awareness of my work and capabilities.

This acceleration happens naturally when you provide genuine value to well-connected individuals. Rather than approaching potential accelerator relationships with calculated intent, focus on creating authentic value. When people genuinely benefit from your contributions, they naturally become advocates and door-openers without requiring deliberate cultivation.

While maintaining an authentic relationship focus, strategically develop connections with those who can amplify your reputation.

These accelerator relationships create compound returns on your relationship investments, extending your reputation far beyond what direct personal effort could achieve.

Brand-Building Through Problem Solving

If you want a personal brand that speaks for itself, become the person who solves problems others can't.

My colleague Michael is the perfect example. He never talked about himself or actively built his "brand," but whenever a complex issue arose, people instinctively turned to him. Why? Because he had built a reputation for figuring things out when no one else could.

Without social media strategies or curated messaging, Michael's name became synonymous with results. And that's the most powerful brand you can have.

The key to Michael's reputation wasn't visibility—it was value. Instead of chasing flashy projects, he focused on solving meaningful problems that impacted the company in a lasting way. Over time, his unique problem-solving approach became his signature—people recognized his name not for what he said, but for what he consistently delivered. His implementation excellence meant consistently executing solutions that worked, not just proposing good ideas without follow-through.

While he didn't engage in deliberate self-promotion, he did create appropriate documentation of results, providing evidence of his effectiveness without excessive claims. Over time, he established clear patterns of problem-solving that people came to rely on, creating a reputation for specific types of solutions.

> **CONNECTION GEM:** *Nothing builds a stronger relationship brand than consistently solving meaningful problems. Focus on addressing challenges that matter rather than seeking brand-building opportunities, and reputation naturally follows.*

This problem-solving approach to reputation building proves particularly effective because it creates tangible value rather than mere impression. The concrete results speak for themselves without requiring elaborate messaging or self-promotion. The reputation emerges naturally from the pattern of solutions rather than from deliberate brand management.

Nothing builds a stronger relationship brand than consistently solving meaningful problems. By focusing on addressing challenges that matter rather than seeking brand-building opportunities, reputation naturally follows success rather than requiring separate cultivation.

Building Brand Through Teaching and Sharing

One of the fastest ways to build a reputation? Teach what you know.

I learned this by accident. I started leading informal workshops, simply sharing what I had learned about cross-industry networking. I wasn't thinking about "branding." But soon, people started associating me with clarity, insight, and connection-building.

And just like that, my expertise became my brand. What started as a simple desire to help others developed into a reputation-defining activity that significantly enhanced my professional opportunities.

Rather than claiming expertise through credentials or self-promotion, these sessions demonstrated capabilities through actual teaching. The genuine value creation—helping others develop their own connection skills—created appreciation that translated into reputation enhancement and new opportunities. Participants particularly valued my ability to make complex networking concepts understandable and practical, building my reputation for clarity and accessibility.

> **CONNECTION GEM:** *Teaching creates relationship-based branding that's both powerful and generous. By helping others develop through your knowledge, you simultaneously demonstrate expertise and create goodwill.*

Consistent contribution through regular knowledge sharing created a reliable pattern that people came to associate with my professional identity. The focus on practical application rather than abstract theory or personal promotion enhanced the value people received and, consequently, their perception of my expertise.

Teaching is branding without bragging. When you help others grow, they don't just remember the knowledge—you become the go-to person for that skill.

That's how you build a personal brand that people respect and trust. The reputation emerges from the value others receive rather than from claims about your capabilities.

This approach proves particularly effective because it shows rather than tells—demonstrating expertise through actual helpful information rather than assertions about qualifications. The goodwill generated through genuine assistance creates advocacy and opportunity through appreciation rather than impression management.

Personal Brand Through Event Creation

You don't have to be the smartest person in the room—just the one who brings the right people together.

Hosting events became one of my most powerful branding tools. By curating high-value gatherings, I positioned myself as a connector, someone who creates opportunities for others. The result? People didn't just remember the events—they remembered me.

My quarterly cross-industry dinners became signature experiences that defined an important aspect of my professional reputation. The distinctive experience design—creating memorable and valuable interactions rather than typical networking events—became associated with my personal brand through consistent participant feedback.

Curation excellence—bringing together complementary participants who wouldn't otherwise connect—created unique value that participants associated directly with my reputation. The value facilitation—enabling meaningful connections and outcomes beyond what attendees could create independently—demonstrated expertise through results rather than claims.

> **CONNECTION GEM:** *Event creation provides unique opportunities for relationship brand development. The experience you create for participants becomes directly associated with your personal reputation.*

Environment creation establishes distinctive atmospheres and settings that participants come to expect and value. Consistent execution delivering reliable quality across multiple gatherings builds trust and anticipation that enhances reputation through reliability.

Event creation provides unique opportunities for relationship brand development because it creates direct, immersive experiences of your capabilities. The gathering you design becomes a three-dimensional demonstration of your values, skills, and expertise, making abstract qualities tangible through concrete experience.

Hosting intentional events builds your brand organically—because people associate the value they gain with the person who made it possible.

Instead of telling people who you are, give them an experience they'll never forget. That's branding at its best.

The Three Reputation Questions

Forget personal brand quizzes—these three questions will tell you everything you need to know. If you want to know how your reputation is working for you (or against you), ask yourself:

The first question—"What do people consistently experience when they interact with you?"—focuses on the actual relationship patterns you create rather than the impression you hope to give. By gathering honest feedback and observing patterns in how others respond to you, you can identify the genuine experience that forms your relationship brand foundation.

The second question—"What do people say about you when you're not in the room?"—addresses the essence of a relationship-based reputation. This isn't about crafted messaging but about the natural discussion that happens based on consistent experience. While difficult to know directly, patterns in how opportunities and introductions come to you often reveal these private perceptions.

The third question—"What opportunities come to you based on reputation rather than pursuit?"—reveals the practical impact of your relationship brand. When people seek you out for specific types of opportunities based on what they've heard about your work, it demonstrates effective reputation development beyond self-promotion.

> **CONNECTION GEM:** *Regularly reflecting on these three questions provides more valuable guidance for relationship-based branding than traditional personal brand assessments. They focus on actual impact rather than projected image.*

Handling Brand Misalignments

Your brand isn't just what you intend—it's what people experience.

I learned this the hard way. A mentor once told me, "You think you're being thorough, but some people feel like you're talking down to them." That wasn't my intention at all—but perception is reality in personal branding.

This misalignment between intention and perception created a brand disconnect that could have undermined my relationship effectiveness if left unaddressed. The experience taught me the importance of perception monitoring—actively seeking and remaining open to honest feedback about how others experience interactions with you, especially when it differs from your intent.

The fix? Adapt, don't overcorrect. Instead of shutting down, I adjusted my approach:

- I started asking before explaining ("Would a detailed breakdown be helpful?").

- I watched for cues—if people seemed engaged, I kept going; if they seemed lost, I simplified.

Small shifts like this make all the difference in how your brand is received.

> **CONNECTION GEM:** *The most valuable brand feedback often comes from misalignments between intention and perception. Remaining open to these insights enables crucial adjustments that strengthen relationship effectiveness.*

Fundamental authenticity remains essential despite adjustments. The goal in addressing misalignments isn't to create an artificial persona, but to ensure your genuine qualities are accurately perceived. This balance between authentic self-expression and thoughtful adjustment based on impact creates the most effective relationship brands.

Brand evolution rather than dramatic reinvention typically creates the most sustainable reputation development. By making incremental adjustments based on feedback while maintaining consistent core attributes, you create relationship brands that evolve naturally rather than confusing connections with disconnected identity shifts.

Chapter Takeaways

1. Authentic personal brands emerge from consistent relationship experiences rather than deliberate image crafting.
2. What others say about you matters more than what you say about yourself.
3. Relationship consistency forms the foundation of powerful personal brands.
4. Problem-solving and knowledge-sharing create particularly valuable reputation enhancement.
5. How you handle challenges often defines your brand more powerfully than successes.
6. Different contexts require adaptations while maintaining authentic core qualities.
7. Relationship-based branding focuses on experience quality rather than messaging volume.

Action Steps

1. **Conduct a Relationship Brand Audit**
   - ☐ Gather feedback about how others experience interactions with you.
   - ☐ Identify consistent patterns in how people describe working with you.
   - ☐ Assess what opportunities come to you based on reputation.
   - ☐ Evaluate alignment between desired and actual relationship brand.
   - ☐ Determine priority development areas,

2. **Develop Your Relationship Consistency**
   - ☐ Identify your core value creation patterns.
   - ☐ Create systems for reliable follow-through.
   - ☐ Establish clear quality standards.
   - ☐ Define non-negotiable behavioral principles.
   - ☐ Build reputation maintenance practices.

3. **Enhance Your Problem-Solving Brand**
   - ☐ Focus on addressing meaningful challenges.
   - ☐ Develop distinctive solution approaches.
   - ☐ Build consistent implementation excellence.
   - ☐ Create appropriate results documentation.
   - ☐ Establish patterns people can rely on.

CHAPTER 8: BUILDING YOUR PERSONAL BRAND THROUGH RELATIONSHIPS

4. **Build Your Knowledge-Sharing Approach**
   - ☐ Identify valuable expertise you can share.
   - ☐ Develop clear teaching and communication methods.
   - ☐ Create regular contribution practices.
   - ☐ Focus on practical application value.
   - ☐ Establish yourself as a generous resource.

5. **Create Your Reputation Ecosystem Map**
   - ☐ Identify direct experience networks.
   - ☐ Map secondary reputation circles.
   - ☐ Assess formal recognition opportunities.
   - ☐ Evaluate content footprint effectiveness.
   - ☐ Align digital presence with relationship brand.

As you develop your relationship-based personal brand, remember that the most powerful reputations emerge from genuine patterns rather than calculated efforts. Focus on creating consistently positive experiences for others, and your personal brand will naturally strengthen over time.

In the next chapter, we'll explore how to convert connections into opportunities—transforming relationships into tangible outcomes that create value for everyone involved.

Final Connection Gem: *At the end of the day, your personal brand isn't what you say. It's what people remember and say about you when you're not in the room. In a world increasingly saturated with personal branding efforts, authentic relationship-based reputation becomes increasingly distinctive and valuable. While others are busy polishing their image, master connectors are out here making an impact. And that's the brand that speaks for itself.*

CHAPTER 9

Converting Connections to Opportunities

"Building connections is just the beginning. The real power of networking emerges when those relationships transform into meaningful opportunities that create value for everyone involved."

The call came out of the blue—or so it seemed. "Nichole," the executive said, "I've been watching the way you connect corporate and creative communities. We need exactly that approach for a major initiative. Would you be interested in leading it?"

It had been three years since we first met. A few emails here, a shared resource there—nothing dramatic. But that slow, steady relationship-building paid off. This wasn't luck. It was relationship conversion at work.

This moment represents what I call "relationship conversion"—the transformation of a connection into a concrete opportunity. The proposal wasn't random or accidental. It emerged from years of consistent relationship nurturing, clear value demonstration, and authentic engagement. I hadn't pushed for this opportunity; I had built the foundation that made it a natural next step.

Many professionals focus intensely on making connections but struggle with the crucial art of converting those relationships into tangible opportunities. They collect contacts at events, build impressive LinkedIn networks, and maintain surface-level relationships—yet wonder why these connections rarely transform into meaningful collaborations, partnerships, or career advancements.

In this chapter, we'll explore the delicate art of relationship conversion—how to transform genuine connections into valuable opportunities without manipulation or pushiness. You'll learn how to naturally evolve relationships toward mutual benefit while maintaining authenticity and trust.

Understanding Relationship Conversion

Relationship conversion is what happens when a connection moves from conversation to collaboration—when someone doesn't just know you but calls on you for an opportunity. Unlike transactional approaches that view relationships primarily as means to predetermined ends, authentic conversion emerges organically from genuinely valuable connections.

CHAPTER 9: CONVERTING CONNECTIONS TO OPPORTUNITIES

The key differences from traditional approaches involve leading with value rather than requests, allowing relationships to develop at an appropriate pace, creating mutual benefit, maintaining a long-term view, and preserving authentic connection throughout.

Early in my career, I watched two people network in completely different ways.

Jamal treated every introduction like a sales pitch—within minutes, he'd ask how they could work together. He made connections quickly but lost them just as fast.

Angela, on the other hand, played the long game. She never asked for favors—she just offered insights, support, and encouragement. For a while, it seemed like her approach was too passive... until the offers started rolling in.

That's when I realized: the best opportunities don't come from chasing. They come from planting the right seeds and letting them grow.

Meanwhile, my mentor Angela built relationships with seemingly limitless patience, focusing entirely on understanding others' goals and offering consistent value without an apparent agenda. I initially worried her approach might be too passive, but I watched in amazement as opportunities flowed to her constantly—often from connections she had nurtured for years without any explicit request.

> **CONNECTION GEM:** *True relationship conversion isn't about "getting something" from your connections—it's about creating the conditions where opportunities naturally emerge from authentic relationship development.*

This observation transformed my understanding of connection conversion. Rather than seeing relationships as transactions to be closed, I began viewing them as gardens to be cultivated—with patience, consistent care, and trust that the harvest would come in its own time. This approach has consistently created more valuable and sustainable opportunities than any direct conversion technique ever could.

The Conversion Mindset

Effective relationship conversion requires a mindset fundamentally different from traditional networking approaches. This mindset begins with patience—understanding that meaningful opportunities often emerge from long-term relationship development rather than immediate conversion efforts. While some connections may yield quick results, the most valuable opportunities typically develop over extended periods as trust and mutual understanding deepen.

A focus on value creation forms the foundation of this mindset—prioritizing what you can contribute to relationships rather than what you can extract from them. By consistently providing benefits without an immediate expectation of return, you build relationship capital that naturally creates opportunity flow over time. This approach reflects abundance thinking rather than a scarcity perspective about professional possibilities.

Pattern recognition represents another crucial mindset element—noticing the natural collaboration potential that emerges through relationship development. As you learn more about others' capabilities, challenges, and goals, you begin recognizing where meaningful connection points might create mutual value without forced opportunity creation.

> **CONNECTION GEM:** *Shift from asking, "What can I get from this relationship?" to "How might value naturally emerge from this connection?" This subtle change transforms how opportunities develop while preserving relationship authenticity.*

Opportunity awareness balances patience with appropriate alertness to natural conversion points. While avoiding premature or forced opportunity pursuit, effective converters maintain sensitivity to moments when relationship evolution naturally suggests potential collaboration. This awareness allows for timely, appropriate opportunity discussion when the relationship has developed sufficiently.

Perhaps most importantly, relationship quality prioritization establishes foundational values for conversion approaches. By valuing connection health above immediate returns, you preserve the trust and authenticity that enable long-term opportunity development. This priority ensures that even when discussing specific possibilities, the relationship itself remains paramount rather than subordinate to the transaction.

The Relationship Value Cycle

Think of relationship conversion like a four-phase cycle:

1. Build the relationship. (Trust first, no agenda.)
2. Show your value. (Share insights, offer help.)
3. Recognize the opportunity. (Listen for their needs.)
4. Make the ask—when it makes sense.

Skip a step? You risk looking pushy or opportunistic. Take your time, and the opportunities will come naturally.

The cycle begins with connection establishment—building initial relationship rapport and understanding. During this phase, focus entirely on establishing an authentic connection without an opportunity agenda. Learn about the person's background, interests, challenges, and goals while sharing your own context appropriately. This foundation creates essential trust for later development.

Value demonstration follows as the relationship develops—consistently providing helpful information, connections, or insights without expecting an immediate return. This contribution builds

CHAPTER 9: CONVERTING CONNECTIONS TO OPPORTUNITIES

relationship capital through genuine service rather than strategically positioned "gifts." The value provided should align with the person's actual needs rather than your conversion agenda.

Trust building forms the critical middle phase where consistent reliability, authentic engagement, and demonstrated competence create the foundation for potential opportunities. This trust develops through multiple positive interactions over time—proving through behavior rather than claims that you can be counted on for both personal integrity and professional capability.

> **CONNECTION GEM:** *Understanding these natural phases prevents premature opportunity pursuit. Each stage builds the foundation for the next, creating sustainable relationship value rather than short-term transactions.*

Opportunity identification emerges naturally as relationship development reveals potential collaboration possibilities. Rather than forcing predetermined opportunities, these possibilities emerge from a genuine understanding of complementary strengths, needs, and goals. The identification often happens mutually as both parties recognize potential value creation through collaboration.

Exploration and definition follow when both parties express interest in the potential opportunity. This phase involves collaborative discussion about how working together might create mutual benefits, defining parameters and expectations through open conversation rather than one-sided proposals. The evolution feels organic rather than forced—a natural next step in relationship development.

Collaboration implementation creates tangible value through actual work together, transforming relationship potential into concrete results. This partnership demonstrates the relationship's capability to generate mutual benefit beyond conversation and connection. The successful collaboration often leads to expanded opportunities as trust and proven value create a foundation for additional possibilities.

Finally, relationship evolution continues the cycle as successful collaboration strengthens connection and creates a foundation for additional opportunities. Rather than viewing any single opportunity as the relationship's purpose, this ongoing evolution maintains connection development beyond specific collaborations, creating sustainable value exchange over time.

A Lesson in Connection Value

One of the most valuable lessons I learned about the monetary worth of connections came through an unexpected interaction with Yandy, a high-profile entrepreneur and media personality in my network.

When ET, a well-known motivational speaker, called asking for help booking talent for his upcoming event, I immediately thought of three influential women in my network—Yandy and

CHAPTER 9: CONVERTING CONNECTIONS TO OPPORTUNITIES

two other high-profile personalities. All three expressed interest in speaking at the event, but Yandy's response taught me something that transformed my understanding of connection value.

Then Yandy hit me with a question I wasn't expecting:

"What's your fee?"

I blinked. "My...what?"

"Nichole, you made this deal happen. You connected the dots. That's worth something. How much are you charging?"

Until that moment, it had never crossed my mind that the introductions I made had monetary value—but to her, it was obvious. "Oh no," I said, somewhat embarrassed. "You don't need to pay me. I'm just making the connection to help you and my friend for his conference."

Yandy looked at me directly and said something I'll never forget: "Nichole, I wouldn't get this deal if it wasn't for you. That's the value of relationship and connection. You should be compensated for that."

She went on to explain that most people in her industry charge anywhere between 5% and 20% for making valuable introductions that lead to business opportunities. Despite being the closest to her out of all three women I'd contacted, I had never considered monetizing the connection.

Yandy insisted on paying me 10% of what she earned from the speaking engagement. This was the first time anyone had shown me that the connections I was creating had tangible monetary value—not just relationship value.

This experience was eye-opening. While I had always understood the professional and personal value of building bridges between people, Yandy helped me recognize that there was also legitimate economic value in the opportunities I was creating through my network. She taught me that being compensated for creating valuable connections wasn't just acceptable—it was expected in many industries.

This lesson was particularly powerful because it came from someone I had a genuine relationship with. Had she been a distant contact or someone I barely knew, I might have dismissed the idea. But, coming from Yandy, whom I respected and had built a real connection with, the message resonated deeply.

This experience fundamentally shifted how I thought about some of my connection activities, helping me recognize when it was appropriate to establish formal business arrangements around certain types of introductions while maintaining the authentic relationship foundation that made those connections valuable in the first place.

Case Study: The Three-Year Conversion

One of my most valuable client relationships developed over three years before our first formal engagement. The relationship began at an industry conference where Mark, a senior executive at a major corporation, participated in a panel discussion on cross-sector collaboration. His thoughtful comments about bridging corporate and community perspectives aligned with my passion for connection across different worlds.

During the reception afterward, I approached him with genuine curiosity about his company's community engagement initiatives rather than any business agenda. Our conversation revealed his frustration with traditional corporate outreach models and his desire for more authentic community connections. Rather than pitching my services, I shared a recent research report on effective cross-sector partnerships that addressed some challenges he'd mentioned.

Two weeks later, I sent a brief follow-up email referencing our conversation and including another relevant resource without asking for anything in return. His appreciative response mentioned ongoing challenges with a specific initiative. Over the following months, I maintained light contact through occasional sharing of relevant information, congratulating him on company announcements, and brief interactions at industry events.

> **CONNECTION GEM:** *Some of the most valuable opportunities come from relationships nurtured without immediate agenda. Patience combined with consistent value demonstration often yields far greater returns than aggressive opportunity pursuit.*

About six months into our connection, Mark mentioned a particularly challenging community engagement issue during a conversation. I offered some perspective based on my experience that he found helpful, which led to a more substantive discussion about his company's approach. Again, I focused on providing valuable insight rather than suggesting formal engagement.

Our relationship continued developing through regular but unforced interaction over the next two years. I attended events where he spoke, shared relevant resources, and occasionally asked for his perspective on industry developments. Throughout this period, I never directly suggested working together, though I was confident my expertise aligned with his company's needs.

Three years after our initial meeting, Mark called to discuss a major initiative his company was launching to transform their community engagement approach. "We need someone who truly understands both corporate and community perspectives," he said. "Your name was the first that came to mind because you've demonstrated that understanding consistently since we met."

The resulting project became one of my most significant client engagements—far more substantial than anything I might have proposed earlier in our relationship. Because it emerged from genuine understanding developed over time, the work aligned perfectly with both my capabilities and his organization's needs, creating exceptional value for everyone involved.

Three years. No pitches. No pressure. Just showing up, providing value, and staying connected. And when the right opportunity came? I was the first person he thought of.

Throughout our three-year connection before formal engagement, my focus remained on relationship building rather than opportunity creation—yet the opportunity that eventually emerged exceeded anything I could have strategically pursued.

Value Demonstration Strategies

Showing your capabilities without overt self-promotion creates natural conversion opportunities. This approach proves far more effective than direct claims about your skills or potential value, as it allows others to experience your capabilities firsthand rather than merely hearing about them.

Problem-solving represents one of the most powerful value demonstration approaches. When my connection Tyler mentioned a challenge his team faced with community participation in their market research, I shared specific suggestions based on my experience. This helpful response demonstrated relevant expertise more effectively than any capabilities statement could have achieved.

Knowledge sharing creates similar demonstration value. When Maria expressed interest in cross-industry collaboration approaches during a conversation, I sent her several case studies and frameworks I'd developed, showcasing my expertise through genuinely useful information rather than credential claims. This natural demonstration created a clear understanding of my capabilities without explicit promotion.

> **CONNECTION GEM:** *The most effective value demonstration comes through authentic help rather than deliberate capability promotion. Focus on creating genuine impact, and the perception of your capabilities naturally follows.*

Connection facilitation powerfully demonstrates your relationship value. When David mentioned needing specialized expertise for a project, I introduced him to someone in my network with exactly the right background. This connection not only helped solve his immediate need but also showcased my network development and connector capabilities—a cornerstone of my professional value.

Demonstrating your capabilities through volunteer contributions creates especially powerful evidence of your expertise as well. When an industry association needed help organizing a complex event, I offered my experience in designing meaningful gatherings. The successful event demonstrated my capabilities to dozens of potential clients more effectively than any marketing could have achieved.

These demonstration approaches share important characteristics: they create genuine value rather than merely positioning capabilities; they showcase relevant expertise through tangible impact rather than claims; and they emerge from an authentic desire to help rather than strategic self-promotion. By focusing on actual contribution, they naturally reveal your capabilities while building the relationship trust that forms the foundation for opportunity development.

The Opportunity Identification Process

Identifying potential collaboration points requires thoughtful relationship observation rather than predetermined opportunity agendas. The foundation begins with comprehensive listening for expressed needs or challenges. During conversations with Taylor, a corporate sustainability director, I noted recurring mentions of difficulty engaging employees in green initiatives. This careful attention revealed an opportunity alignment with my engagement expertise that might have remained hidden without attentive listening.

Capability-need alignment provides the crucial connection between what you offer and what others require. After several conversations with Marcus about his company's community outreach challenges, I recognized how my cross-sector facilitation experience directly addressed his specific needs. This natural alignment created obvious value potential without requiring opportunity manipulation.

> **CONNECTION GEM:** *Effective opportunity identification involves listening more than speaking. The most valuable collaboration possibilities often emerge from careful attention to stated challenges rather than aggressive opportunity promotion.*

Timing sensitivity proves essential for appropriate opportunity identification. When Sarah mentioned her organization was beginning strategic planning for next year's initiatives, it signaled perfect timing for potential collaboration discussions. Recognizing these natural timing windows helps identify when relationship development has reached appropriate stages for opportunity exploration.

Value gap identification creates particularly meaningful opportunity recognition. Through a conversation with Carlos about his market expansion strategy, I noticed a specific expertise gap in community engagement that my knowledge could address. This clear value gap made potential collaboration obvious without requiring opportunity manufacturing.

The most important aspect of opportunity identification is its natural emergence from genuine relationship development. Rather than approaching connections with predetermined opportunities to pursue, effective converters allow potential collaboration to reveal itself through a developing understanding of others' needs, challenges, and goals. This organic identification creates opportunities aligned with actual needs rather than forced collaboration that might not serve genuine interests.

The Art of the Natural Proposition

When the time is right to propose potential collaboration, specific approaches create more effective conversion without compromising relationship authenticity. The foundation begins with value-centered framing that focuses on benefits for the other person rather than your own interests. When discussing potential work with Elena after months of relationship development, I began with, "Based on the challenges you've mentioned with cross-departmental collaboration, I believe I could help create more effective integration through..." This framing centered on her needs rather than my desire for the opportunity.

Conversation orientation maintains dialogue rather than presentation during opportunity discussion. Instead of delivering a formal pitch to Jordan about potential collaboration, I suggested, "exploring whether my community engagement approach might help address the challenges you've mentioned." This conversational framing invited collaborative exploration rather than creating sales pressure.

> **CONNECTION GEM:** *The most effective opportunity propositions feel like natural relationship evolutions rather than sales pitches. When presented appropriately, collaboration feels like an obvious next step rather than an unexpected request.*

Mutual benefit emphasis ensures balanced value exchange in opportunity discussions. When proposing a potential workshop series to Kimberly's organization, I explicitly outlined benefits for both her team and mine rather than focusing solely on what I could provide. This mutual value focus maintained relationship equality rather than creating a provider-client imbalance.

Timing appropriateness remains crucial for effective propositions. Rather than raising potential collaboration during initial meetings with William, I waited until our relationship had developed through multiple value exchanges and his needs were clearly understood. This appropriate timing ensured the opportunity discussion felt like a natural evolution rather than a premature agenda.

Perhaps most importantly, authentic connection maintenance preserves relationship quality during opportunity discussions. Even while exploring potential collaboration with Rebecca, I made clear that our relationship value extended beyond any specific opportunity. This genuine connection emphasis prevented the relationship from becoming purely transactional regardless of the proposition's outcome.

CHAPTER 9: CONVERTING CONNECTIONS TO OPPORTUNITIES

These natural proposition approaches transform opportunity discussions from awkward sales conversations to organic relationship evolutions. By maintaining focus on genuine value, collaborative exploration, and relationship quality above transaction, they create opportunity conversion that strengthens rather than compromises authentic connection.

The Three Conversion Questions

Three key questions have guided my approach to effective relationship conversion throughout my career. When thoughtfully considered before attempting opportunity development, they help ensure both appropriate timing and an authentic approach.

The first question—Is this the right time? (Or am I rushing it?)—addresses crucial timing considerations. By evaluating the relationship development stage, trust establishment, value exchange history, and mutual understanding depth, you can determine whether a sufficient foundation exists for a natural opportunity discussion. Premature exploration often damages developing connections, while appropriate timing enhances relationships through natural evolution.

The second question— How does this benefit them? (Not just me.) —focuses on genuine benefit creation rather than generic opportunity pursuit. By identifying particular needs or challenges the relationship could address, specific capabilities that create meaningful impact, and unique perspective advantages collaboration might offer, you ensure that any opportunity discussion centers on authentic value rather than manufactured possibilities.

> **CONNECTION GEM:** *Regularly reflecting on these questions prevents premature or inappropriate conversion attempts. They focus on relationship readiness and mutual value rather than one-sided opportunity extraction.*

The third question—"How can this opportunity benefit everyone involved?"—ensures balanced value creation essential for sustainable opportunity development. By considering multiple stakeholder perspectives, various benefit dimensions beyond immediate outcomes, and potential challenges that might create imbalance, you develop opportunities that strengthen rather than exploit relationships.

These questions transform opportunity development from self-interested transaction pursuit to mutual value creation through authentic relationship evolution. By consistently applying them before conversion attempts, you develop opportunities that emerge naturally from meaningful connections rather than forced transactions that compromise relationship quality.

Digital Relationship Conversion

Online relationships require specific approaches to opportunity development. These digital connections often follow different development patterns than in-person relationships, requiring thoughtful adaptation of conversion principles rather than simply transferring physical-world approaches to online contexts.

The foundation begins with progressive relationship development across platforms. My connection with Nasir began through LinkedIn comments on his industry articles, evolved to direct messages sharing relevant resources, developed through video conversations about shared interests, and eventually led to in-person meetings that created the foundation for collaboration. This gradual platform progression built sufficient relationship depth for meaningful opportunity development, despite beginning entirely online.

Content value demonstration creates particularly effective digital conversion paths. By consistently sharing genuinely helpful content relevant to Sophia's expressed challenges, I established clear capability demonstration without explicit promotion. This ongoing value provision created a natural foundation for opportunity discussion when her needs aligned with my demonstrated expertise.

> **CONNECTION GEM:** *Digital relationships often require more progressive relationship building before opportunity exploration. The absence of physical interaction typically necessitates more extensive trust development stages.*

Platform-appropriate communication respect recognizes different conversion approaches for various digital environments.

While LinkedIn might support relatively direct professional opportunity discussions after sufficient relationship development, similar directness on social platforms like Instagram would likely feel inappropriate without extensive relationship establishment. Understanding these contextual differences prevents premature or misaligned conversion attempts.

In-person transition creates particularly valuable conversion opportunities for relationships begun online. After developing a substantial digital connection with Marcus through multiple video conversations and resource exchanges, our first in-person meeting at an industry conference created a natural opportunity to discuss potential collaboration. This physical interaction often accelerates relationship development that enables more meaningful opportunity exploration.

Patience becomes especially important in digital relationship conversion. Without the immediacy and multi-dimensional information exchange of physical interaction, online relationships typically require more time and interaction touchpoints to develop sufficient trust for opportunity exploration. This extended timeline requires greater discipline to avoid premature conversion attempts that might damage developing connections.

These digital principles adapt core conversion concepts to online relationship realities while maintaining the fundamental focus on authentic development, genuine value creation, and appropriate timing essential for effective opportunity emergence. By respecting the unique development patterns of digital relationships, you can create meaningful conversion opportunities even without traditional in-person connection advantages.

Industry-Specific Conversion Approaches

Different professional contexts require tailored conversion strategies that respect the norms and expectations of each field. Corporate environments typically value formal processes, established frameworks, and clear value propositions in opportunity development. When discussing potential collaboration with financial institution executives, I ensured our exploration followed structured evaluation processes familiar in their industry rather than the more organic approaches that might work elsewhere.

Entrepreneurial settings generally prefer direct, innovative, and flexible opportunity approaches. My conversations with startup founders about potential collaboration emphasized creative possibilities, adaptable parameters, and swift exploration rather than the formal processes appropriate in corporate contexts. This approach alignment created comfortable conversion discussions suited to the entrepreneurial culture.

> **CONNECTION GEM:** *While maintaining authentic core principles, adapt conversion timing and approaches to industry norms. Understanding context-specific expectations helps relationships evolve naturally within different professional environments.*

Creative industries typically value personal connection, shared vision, and collaborative exploration in opportunity development. My work with entertainment industry professionals emphasized relationship authenticity, creative alignment, and vision sharing rather than structured proposals or formal business cases. This approach honored the relationship primacy characteristic of creative fields.

Professional services often expect credential establishment, methodological clarity, and expertise demonstration before opportunity discussions. When developing relationships with legal or consulting professionals, I emphasized relevant experience, clear methodologies, and established protocols that aligned with their field's approach to new engagements.

Community organizations typically prioritize mission alignment, authentic commitment, and collaborative values in opportunity development. My work with nonprofit leaders focused on shared purpose, community benefit, and collaborative approach rather than business metrics or procedural formality that might seem misaligned with their organizational culture.

These adaptations maintain core conversion principles—authentic relationship development, genuine value creation, appropriate timing—while honoring the cultural contexts that shape different professional environments. By understanding and respecting these industry-specific expectations, you create opportunity discussions that feel natural and appropriate within each relationship context rather than imposing standardized approaches regardless of the setting.

The Introduction as Opportunity Creation

Strategic introductions can create powerful conversion possibilities for everyone involved. This approach often generates more substantial opportunities than direct collaboration, positioning you as a valuable connector while creating potential for three-way partnership development.

The foundation begins with complementary need-resource matching between connections. When I recognized that Amir's technology expertise perfectly addressed Rebecca's organization's digital challenges, introducing them created immediate value for both while establishing my connector value. These targeted introductions based on specific alignment create far more impact than generic networking connections.

Mutual benefit articulation creates particularly effective introductions. When connecting James with Sophia, I explicitly outlined potential advantages for both—how James's community access could enhance Sophia's research while her institutional resources could support his program development. This clear value articulation for both parties established purpose beyond simple networking.

> **CONNECTION GEM:** *Introduction facilitation often creates more valuable opportunities than direct conversion. By connecting others strategically, you develop a reputation as a valuable relationship hub while creating potential collaborative possibilities.*

Thoughtful preparation ensures introduction effectiveness. Before connecting Carlos with Elizabeth, I confirmed with each that the introduction aligned with their current priorities and provided contextual information that established immediate relevance. This preparation transformed the introduction from potentially awkward networking to a purposeful connection with clear value potential.

Meaningful engagement support helps connections develop beyond the initial introduction. After connecting Miguel with Sarah, I suggested specific follow-up possibilities and offered to coordinate initial conversations if helpful. This support ensured the introduction developed into meaningful engagement rather than just adding to contact lists.

Three-way collaboration potential creates particularly valuable introduction opportunities. By connecting Diana's research expertise with Robert's implementation capabilities to address marketplace challenges we had all discussed separately, I created three-way partnership potential that benefited everyone while establishing central connector value beyond the introduction itself.

CHAPTER 9: CONVERTING CONNECTIONS TO OPPORTUNITIES

These strategic introductions transform opportunity creation from direct pursuit to facilitated connection that positions you as a valuable network hub. By thoughtfully connecting others in ways that create mutual benefit, you establish yourself as someone who generates opportunity through relationships rather than simply seeking personal advantage.

Navigating Conversion Challenges

Even thoughtful conversion approaches sometimes face obstacles that require skillful navigation to preserve both opportunity potential and relationship quality. Timing misalignment represents one common challenge—when relationships aren't ready for opportunities despite apparent value potential. When I recognized that my connection with Alexander wasn't sufficiently developed for the collaboration possibility I envisioned, I deliberately postponed the opportunity discussion while continuing relationship nurturing. This patience preserved connection quality while creating a stronger foundation for later exploration.

Value perception differences create another frequent challenge—when parties see potential collaboration value differently. Rather than pushing my perspective when Jennifer didn't immediately recognize the opportunity value I perceived, I asked questions to better understand her viewpoint and adapt the possibility of framing to address her specific priorities. This collaborative exploration created shared understanding rather than competing perspectives.

> **CONNECTION GEM:** *How you handle conversion challenges often determines relationship longevity. Respectful navigation of obstacles demonstrates professionalism and preserves connection value beyond immediate opportunities.*

Personal-professional boundary navigation requires particular sensitivity. When my relationship with Thomas included both friendship and potential professional collaboration, I explicitly discussed how we might manage both dimensions to ensure neither compromised the other. This boundary clarity preserved relationship quality regardless of opportunity decisions.

Collaboration fit demands thoughtful exploration. When Marcus expressed hesitation about whether our working styles would align effectively, I suggested a small initial project rather than full engagement to test compatibility with limited risk. This graduated approach addressed legitimate concerns while creating an opportunity for successful demonstration.

Competition potential arises when opportunity exploration reveals potential conflicts with existing relationships. When I recognized potential overlap between a new opportunity with Christina's organization and my established work with a similar company, I transparently discussed the situation with both parties to determine appropriate boundaries. This ethical clarity preserved trust while enabling appropriate opportunity development.

These navigation approaches maintain relationship quality while addressing legitimate conversion challenges. By approaching obstacles with respect, transparency, and collaboration rather than manipulation or pressure, you preserve connection value regardless of immediate opportunity outcomes. This relationship prioritization often leads to future possibilities even when specific opportunities aren't initially realized.

Measuring Conversion Effectiveness

Assessing relationship conversion helps refine your approach by identifying patterns in what creates sustainable opportunity development. Rather than focusing solely on conversion quantities, effective assessment examines relationship and opportunity quality through multiple dimensions.

The foundation begins with value creation evaluation across all parties. Beyond my own benefit from collaboration with healthcare organizations, I assess how our work enhances their mission effectiveness, participant outcomes, and organizational capabilities. This comprehensive value assessment ensures genuine mutual benefit rather than one-sided advantage.

Relationship impact assessment examines how opportunity pursuit affects connection quality. Following collaboration discussions with technology partners, I evaluate whether our relationship has strengthened through shared purpose, remained stable despite potential challenges, or diminished through opportunity focus.

This relationship prioritization ensures opportunity pursuit enhances rather than damages valuable connections.

> **CONNECTION GEM:** *Effective conversion measurement focuses on relationship quality alongside opportunity outcomes. The best conversions strengthen connections while creating value, rather than extracting benefit at the relationship's expense.*

Process naturalness evaluation considers whether opportunity development felt organic rather than forced. After successful project initiation with community partners, I reflect on whether our collaboration emerged through mutual recognition of potential value or required significant persuasion despite apparent alignment. This process quality assessment helps refine future approach authenticity.

Continued collaboration potential examines opportunities for ongoing partnership beyond initial engagement. Rather than viewing my work with educational institutions as isolated projects, I assess foundation development for extended relationship value through multiple collaborations. This continuing potential focus creates sustainable opportunity development rather than transactional extraction.

Reputation effect monitoring evaluates how opportunity conversion influences broader professional perception. Beyond immediate outcomes from corporate partnerships, I consider how our collaboration approach shapes perception among potential partners who observe our engagement. This reputation consciousness ensures conversion approaches enhance rather than damage professional standing.

These assessment dimensions create a comprehensive conversion evaluation beyond simple metrics like opportunity quantities or revenue generation. By examining relationship quality, process authenticity, and sustainable value creation alongside traditional outcome measures, you develop increasingly effective approaches that generate opportunities while enhancing your most valuable professional asset—authentic relationships that create ongoing value.

Chapter Takeaways

1. The most valuable opportunities typically emerge from patient relationship development rather than aggressive conversion.
2. Authentic value demonstration creates more powerful conversion potential than direct capability claims.
3. Different relationship types and industries require tailored conversion approaches.
4. Strategic introductions often create more valuable opportunities than direct conversion.
5. In appropriate professional contexts, recognizing the monetary value of your connection-making abilities is legitimate and expected.

6. Effective conversion strengthens rather than compromises relationship quality.
7. The most natural opportunities emerge from genuine alignment rather than forced connections.

Action Steps

1. **Conduct a Relationship Portfolio Review**
   - ☐ Assess current connections and their development stages.
   - ☐ Identify relationships with natural collaboration potential.
   - ☐ Evaluate conversion readiness across your network.
   - ☐ Determine appropriate next steps for key relationships.
   - ☐ Create relationship development priorities.

2. **Develop Your Value Demonstration Strategy**
   - ☐ Identify your most valuable capabilities and knowledge.
   - ☐ Create approaches for showcasing these through genuine help.
   - ☐ Build systematic value provision approaches.
   - ☐ Establish consistency in capability demonstration.
   - ☐ Develop measurement for value impact.

3. **Create Your Opportunity Identification Framework**
    - ☐ Build active listening approaches for need recognition.
    - ☐ Develop capability alignment awareness.
    - ☐ Create timing sensitivity for opportunity exploration.
    - ☐ Establish value gap perception capabilities.
    - ☐ Build convergence spotting approaches.
4. **Design Your Natural Proposition Strategy**
    - ☐ Develop value-centered opportunity framing.
    - ☐ Create conversational introduction approaches.
    - ☐ Build mutual benefit articulation capabilities.
    - ☐ Establish timing appropriateness guidelines.
    - ☐ Develop authentic presentation techniques.

As you develop your relationship conversion capabilities, remember that the most valuable opportunities typically emerge from genuine connections rather than calculated networking. Focus on building authentic relationships and consistently demonstrating value, and conversion opportunities will naturally follow.

In the next chapter, we'll explore digital age networking—how to build meaningful connections in online environments while maintaining the authenticity that creates powerful relationships.

> **Final Connection Gem:** *In a professional world often characterized by transactional networking and immediate gratification, the patient art of relationship conversion creates increasingly rare and valuable opportunities. By focusing on authentic connection development rather than aggressive opportunity extraction, you build not just immediate collaboration but sustainable relationship capital that provides compounding returns over time.*

CHAPTER 10

Digital Age Networking

> *"The most powerful digital connections aren't created through algorithms but through authentic human engagement that happens to use technology as its medium."*

The message arrived in my LinkedIn inbox late one evening: "Nichole, I've been following your content about cross-industry collaboration for months. Your approach to connecting corporate and creative worlds aligns perfectly with a major initiative we're launching. Would you be open to a conversation about potentially partnering?"

This wasn't a random outreach. The sender had thoughtfully engaged with my content over time, leaving insightful comments, sharing relevant resources, and gradually building a relationship before suggesting collaboration. What followed was a partnership that created significant value for both our organizations—a relationship that began entirely in the digital realm before transitioning to in-person collaboration.

This experience illustrates a crucial truth about effective networking in the digital age: While technology has transformed how we connect, the fundamental principles of authentic relationship building remain unchanged. The most valuable digital connections aren't created through aggressive outreach or algorithmic matching but through genuine engagement that happens to use technology as its medium.

In this chapter, we'll explore how to build meaningful, valuable relationships in digital environments. We'll examine how to leverage various platforms while avoiding the transactional approaches that plague so much online networking. Whether you're building connections through social media, virtual events, online communities, or digital content, you'll discover how to create authentic relationships that transcend the limitations of screen-based interaction.

Understanding the Digital Connection Landscape

Digital networking offers unique characteristics that distinguish it from traditional in-person networking. It provides scalable possibilities, allowing you to establish far more connections than physical networking permits. It grants geographic freedom, enabling relationship building unrestricted by location. Digital environments offer asynchronous engagement, letting connections develop without requiring simultaneous availability. They provide content leverage, using created materials to attract aligned relationships. And they enhance visibility, building a presence that extends beyond direct connections.

These capabilities create extraordinary relationship development potential when approached with authentic connection principles. In my own experience, digital platforms have allowed me to develop meaningful professional relationships with people across continents, time zones, and industry boundaries that would have been impossible through traditional networking alone.

But digital networking comes with its own set of traps:

- You can make a thousand connections—but how many are real relationships?
- You can talk to people anywhere in the world—but do you understand their context and culture?
- You can create an impressive online presence—but does it truly reflect who you are?

Asynchronous engagement might produce disjointed communication without consistent attention. Content leverage risks crafting artificial personas disconnected from the authentic self. And enhanced visibility sometimes generates impression management rather than genuine relationship development.

> **CONNECTION GEM:** *Digital networking isn't simply traditional networking moved online—it has fundamentally different dynamics and possibilities. Understanding these distinctions helps you leverage digital environments' unique advantages rather than merely replicating physical networking approaches online.*

The key to effective digital networking lies in harnessing these unique characteristics while maintaining the authentic connection principles that create meaningful relationships in any environment. By understanding both the distinctive opportunities and challenges digital platforms present, you can develop approaches that leverage technological advantages without sacrificing the relationship quality essential for valuable connection development.

The Digital Connection Mindset

Effective online relationship building requires specific mental approaches that adapt authentic connection principles to digital environments. The foundation begins with authentic engagement—viewing digital platforms as relationship environments rather than broadcast channels. When I first joined LinkedIn, I observed many professionals using it primarily to distribute promotional content about themselves. Meanwhile, others approached the same platform as a community for thoughtful exchange and genuine connection building. The relationship results of these different approaches proved dramatically different.

A value-first orientation maintains even greater importance online than in physical networking. With digital environments' lower interaction barriers, countless connection requests and messages compete for attention. By leading with authentic value—sharing helpful information, offering thoughtful perspectives, and making relevant introductions—you immediately distinguish yourself from transactional networkers who begin relationships with requests or self-promotion.

> **CONNECTION GEM:** *Stop treating digital platforms like megaphones. Start using them like living rooms. The best connections don't come from shouting about your success—they come from real conversations, valuable insights, and authentic engagement.*

Progressive development understanding recognizes that digital relationships evolve through stages rather than forming instantaneously. Just as physical relationships develop gradually through repeated positive interactions, meaningful online connections require progressive trust-building through consistent value exchange. This developmental perspective prevents the common mistake of treating digital connections as immediately equivalent to established in-person relationships, despite their relatively nascent development.

The integration perspective sees online and offline connections as complementary dimensions of unified relationships rather than separate networking realms. Rather than maintaining distinct "online" and "real-world" personas, effective digital connectors maintain a consistent authentic presence across environments, recognizing that relationship value emerges from integrated connection rather than compartmentalized engagement.

The long-term vision maintains focus on building enduring digital presence and relationships rather than pursuing viral moments or temporary visibility. This patient perspective recognizes that meaningful online relationships, like their physical counterparts, develop through consistent value provision over time rather than isolated impressive interactions. The most valuable digital connections I've built have emerged through years of consistent engagement rather than dramatic short-term initiatives.

This digital connection mindset transforms online networking from tactical platform manipulation to authentic relationship development that happens to occur through technological mediums. By approaching digital environments with the same fundamental principles that guide valuable in-person connections—authenticity, value creation, progressive development, and long-term perspective—you build relationships that transcend screen limitations to create genuine professional value.

Case Study: Content-Driven Relationship Development

One of my most valuable business relationships began through thoughtful content engagement that evolved into meaningful

CHAPTER 10: DIGITAL AGE NETWORKING

collaboration, despite beginning entirely online. The relationship with Ken, a corporate innovation leader, demonstrates how digital connections can develop progressively when approached with authentic engagement principles rather than transactional networking tactics.

It all started with one post. Ken, a corporate innovation leader, found my article through an industry hashtag on LinkedIn. He didn't send a connection request right away. Instead, he engaged—leaving insightful comments, sharing my content, and adding his own perspective to discussions. My article about bridging corporate and creative worlds to drive innovation aligned with challenges he faced in his organization, causing him to follow my profile for additional insights. At this stage, no direct interaction had occurred—he was simply consuming content that provided value for his professional interests.

His consistent engagement through thoughtful comments and shares over several months created initial connection points. Rather than merely clicking "like," he contributed substantive perspective to discussions, demonstrating genuine interest in the topics rather than performative networking. This meaningful engagement naturally drew my attention, leading me to review his profile and discover potential connection value beyond comment exchanges.

> **CONNECTION GEM:** *Digital relationships often follow a natural progression from passive content consumption to active engagement to direct interaction to eventual collaboration. Respecting and facilitating this evolution typically yields stronger connections than forcing premature advancement.*

Direct interaction followed through private message exchanges about specific shared interests. After noticing his consistent thoughtful engagement, I sent a connection request with a personalized message referencing specific points he had contributed to discussions. This personalization demonstrated genuine interest in connection rather than mass networking accumulation. Our subsequent message exchanges explored common professional interests with increasingly substantive discussions.

Value exchange developed as we began sharing relevant resources and connections with each other. He provided industry reports relevant to my client work; I shared case studies addressing innovation challenges he had mentioned. This reciprocal value provision created relationship substance beyond surface-level digital connection, establishing a meaningful professional bond despite having never met in person.

Collaboration exploration emerged through a virtual meeting to discuss potential partnership. After several months of digital relationship development, we scheduled a video call to explore how our complementary expertise might address specific challenges. This conversation felt natural rather than forced precisely because a sufficient relationship foundation had developed through progressive digital engagement.

Physical transition happened when we finally met in person at an industry conference. Despite being our first face-to-face meeting, it felt like reconnecting with an established colleague rather than meeting a stranger. The digital relationship foundation created immediate comfort and connection that would have required multiple in-person interactions to develop otherwise.

Ongoing partnership developed with successful collaboration that continues to create value for both our organizations. What began as a content-driven digital connection evolved into a meaningful professional relationship generating significant business opportunities and knowledge exchange. This progression from content consumption to valuable partnership exemplifies the potential for authentic digital relationships when developed with appropriate progressive engagement rather than transactional networking tactics.

Platform Selection Strategy

Different digital environments serve different networking purposes, making strategic selection crucial for effective relationship development. My most valuable connections have emerged through deliberate platform choices aligned with specific relationship goals rather than attempts at omnipresence across all digital environments.

Not every platform is for every purpose.

Here's where to focus:

- LinkedIn: Best for professional networking and industry insights.
- Instagram & TikTok: Great for creative fields and lifestyle branding.
- Twitter (X): Best for thought leadership, quick engagement, and industry news.
- Facebook Groups & Forums: Ideal for niche communities and long-form discussions.

Instead of trying to be everywhere, be strategic. Choose one or two platforms where your audience is—and go deep. My most valuable client and strategic partner relationships have overwhelmingly begun through these professionally oriented platforms rather than general social media.

Visual platforms like Instagram suit creative and lifestyle relationships. These visually focused environments facilitate connection through aesthetic expression, behind-the-scenes glimpses, and lifestyle demonstration. My relationships with creative professionals—designers, photographers, event specialists—often develop more effectively through these visually rich platforms that showcase creative perspectives better than text-focused environments.

CHAPTER 10: DIGITAL AGE NETWORKING

> **CONNECTION GEM:** *Rather than trying to maintain a strong presence across all platforms, strategic specialization creates more effective digital networking. Focus your primary efforts on environments that best match your relationship goals and natural communication style.*

Twitter and content platforms facilitate idea-based networking. These discussion-oriented environments create connections through thought exchange, perspective sharing, and intellectual engagement. My relationships with thought leaders, researchers, and subject matter experts often begin through these idea-focused platforms that allow substantive concept exploration before direct relationship development.

Facebook groups and forums excel in shared-interest connection. These community-oriented environments create relationships through common passions, mutual support, and collaborative learning. My connections with like-minded professionals pursuing specific methodologies or addressing particular challenges often develop most naturally through these interest-focused communities.

Emerging platforms offer unique connection approaches for specialized interaction. New digital environments continuously create innovative relationship development possibilities through distinctive features and evolving community norms. By remaining aware of platform evolution while focusing primary energy on established environments most aligned with your connection goals, you maintain both stability and adaptability in your digital networking approach.

The most effective platform selection strategy focuses resources on environments that best serve your specific relationship development goals rather than attempting equal presence across all digital spaces. By understanding different platforms' distinct networking characteristics and aligning your engagement accordingly, you create more meaningful connections than platform-agnostic approaches typically achieve.

Content as Connection Catalyst

Thoughtfully created materials can attract and develop valuable relationships when approached with genuine value provision rather than self-promotion. This content-driven connection strategy has transformed my own networking approach from active outreach to the magnetic attraction of aligned professionals seeking meaningful engagement.

Value-first content that provides genuinely helpful information without requiring immediate return creates a powerful relationship foundation. My most effective connection-building materials focus entirely on solving specific problems or addressing particular challenges my ideal connections face, demonstrating capability through actual help rather than claimed expertise. This problem-solving orientation attracts precisely the relationships I value most while establishing an authentic connection foundation through actual contribution.

Distinctive viewpoint demonstration establishes your unique perspective and approach without explicit self-promotion. Rather than generic content that could come from anyone in your field, materials expressing your particular understanding and methodologies naturally attract aligned professionals who resonate with your approach. My content about bridging different professional worlds attracts precisely the cross-sector collaborators I most enjoy working with based on natural resonance rather than targeted outreach.

> **CONNECTION GEM:** *Your content should be a magnet—not a megaphone.*
>
> - Solve real problems. (People connect with solutions, not self-promotion.)
> - Show your unique perspective. (Be different, not just informative.)
> - Start conversations. (Ask questions. Invite engagement.)
>
> The more value you create, the more people will come to you.

Conversation initiation through content that naturally sparks engagement creates relationship development opportunities. Materials that ask thoughtful questions, present intriguing perspectives, or offer unexpected insights naturally generate meaningful discussion rather than passive consumption. These dialogue-generating approaches transform content from broadcast to conversation, creating natural relationship development pathways without forced networking tactics.

Trust-building through consistent, reliable presence demonstrates dependability essential for meaningful connection. Regular valuable content—whether weekly articles, monthly analyses, or quarterly in-depth explorations—creates relationship continuity despite limited direct interaction. This consistent presence establishes reliability that forms the foundation for deeper engagement when direct connection opportunities emerge.

Natural relationship evolution facilitation using content that progressively deepens engagement creates sustainable connection development. Beginning with broadly helpful materials before gradually introducing more specialized content allows relationships to evolve naturally from initial awareness to substantive engagement based on demonstrated value rather than claimed capabilities. This progressive approach respects digital relationship development stages rather than attempting immediate deep connection through premature intimacy.

The most powerful content-driven networking approaches focus entirely on creating genuine value for potential connections rather than promoting yourself or manufacturing engagement. By consistently providing materials that actually help your ideal professional relationships, you naturally attract and develop valuable connections without requiring aggressive outreach or manipulative tactics that characterize much digital networking.

> **CONNECTION GEM:** *Five real connections are better than 500 empty ones. Instead of "liking" posts mindlessly, try leaving a thoughtful comment, sending a quick voice message, or asking a genuine question. Digital networking is about depth, not just reach.*

Valuable contributions through meaningful insights added to discussions create relationship value through actual help rather than networking positioning. Sharing relevant experiences, offering helpful resources, or providing useful perspectives within conversations demonstrates both expertise and generosity more effectively than claimed capabilities or strategic positioning. This value-driven engagement builds relationship capital through genuine contributions rather than manufactured impressions.

Consistent presence through reliable interaction establishes dependability essential for meaningful digital relationships. Regular, thoughtful engagement—even if relatively infrequent—creates a more valuable connection than sporadic intensive networking followed by absence. My own most valuable online relationships have developed through consistent moderate engagement rather than intermittent aggressive connection attempts that characterize tactical networking approaches.

A personal-professional balance appropriate to specific platform norms creates an authentic presence without inappropriate disclosure. Different digital environments have distinct expectations regarding personal sharing within professional relationships. Understanding these contextual norms while maintaining a consistent core identity across platforms creates authentic engagement that respects both relationship development and platform-appropriate boundaries.

These engagement approaches transform digital interaction from tactical networking performance to authentic relationship development that happens to occur online. By focusing on creating genuine value through thoughtful digital engagement rather than manufacturing connection through strategic performance, you build meaningful relationships that transcend platform limitations to create valuable professional connections.

The Cold Outreach Challenge

Initiating new digital relationships presents particular challenges requiring specific approaches to create connections without appearing transactional or intrusive. Having both received countless ineffective outreach attempts and developed successful connection initiation approaches, I've identified specific strategies that transform cold digital outreach from networking irritation to welcome relationship initiation.

CHAPTER 10: DIGITAL AGE NETWORKING

Connection point identification through shared contacts provides crucial context for new relationship initiation. Beginning outreach with "I noticed we're both connected with [mutual contact]" creates immediate relevance through an established relationship rather than a random connection attempt. This shared connection reference establishes an indirect trust foundation that significantly enhances response likelihood compared to entirely cold outreach.

Specific benefit leading rather than generic networking creates immediate value perception. Beginning with "I saw your question about cross-sector collaboration and have experience that might help" provides clear relevance and potential value rather than vague networking interest. This specific value proposition transforms outreach from a perceived imposition to a welcome offer, dramatically increasing positive response likelihood.

> **CONNECTION GEM:** *No one likes getting a copy-paste message. Instead of saying "Hey, I'd love to connect!", try: "I saw your post on [topic], and it really resonated. I'd love to hear your thoughts on [related topic]" or "We have a mutual connection, [name], and I've admired your work in [industry]. I would love to chat!"*

Make your outreach about them—not just you.

Genuine research demonstration through specific personalization establishes authentic interest rather than a mass outreach impression. Referencing particular content they've created, specific professional achievements, or unique aspects of their work demonstrates actual interest in them as individuals rather than generic networking targets. This demonstrated research creates perceived respectful attention that enhances connection potential.

Proportional request sizing ensures that requests are appropriate to the relationship stage. Initial outreach requesting brief perspective sharing rather than an extended meeting or significant assistance respects relationship development stages rather than prematurely seeking depth inappropriate to connection development. These appropriately sized initial requests create a comfortable engagement opportunity without relationship overreach.

Persistent but respectful follow-up balances determination with consideration. A single additional outreach after a non-response demonstrates interest without creating pressure or annoyance. This balanced persistence acknowledges potential message oversight without assuming entitlement to a response that characterizes problematic networking approaches.

These strategies transform cold digital outreach from networking annoyance to a welcome connection opportunity. By focusing entirely on creating value for the recipient rather than seeking immediate benefit for yourself, you establish initial digital relationships that can develop into meaningful professional connections despite beginning without established relationship context.

The Privacy-Connection Balance

Effective digital networking requires thoughtful personal information management that balances relationship development with appropriate protection. Having navigated these considerations throughout my career while building valuable online relationships, I've developed approaches that create meaningful connections without compromising personal security or comfort.

Limitation determination based on a thoughtful assessment of potential risks creates the foundation for appropriate digital sharing. Identifying specific information categories that present particular concerns—home location details, family members' names, financial specifics—establishes clear boundaries for online disclosure, regardless of the relationship development stage. These predetermined limitations prevent incremental boundary erosion that sometimes occurs without explicit consideration.

Progressive disclosure aligned with relationship development stages maintains appropriate privacy while allowing authentic connection. Sharing general professional background before specific career details and personal context creates a natural information progression that mirrors in-person relationship development rather than either withholding essential connection context or prematurely sharing inappropriate personal details.

> **CONNECTION GEM:** *Digital relationship building requires more deliberate privacy management than in-person connection. Thoughtful approaches allow authentic engagement while maintaining appropriate personal boundaries.*

Platform-specific sharing calibration acknowledges different environments' distinct privacy implications. Recognizing that information shared on professionally oriented platforms like LinkedIn creates different exposure than content on more personal environments like Facebook allows context-appropriate disclosure that respects both platform norms and personal comfort. This calibrated approach prevents inappropriate cross-context information flow while maintaining an authentic presence within each environment.

Balance maintenance between protection needs and connection benefits requires ongoing consideration rather than rigid rules. Different professional contexts, relationship types, and personal circumstances create varying appropriate disclosure levels that require thoughtful assessment rather than universal guidelines. This flexible approach allows privacy protection without unnecessary connection limitation through excessive restriction.

These balanced approaches create appropriate digital disclosure that facilitates meaningful relationship development without compromising personal security or comfort. By thoughtfully managing what information you share, with whom, in what contexts, and at what relationship stages, you create an authentic online presence that enables valuable connection while maintaining appropriate personal boundaries.

Digital Personal Branding Through Relationships

Online reputation develops primarily through interaction patterns rather than deliberate image creation. Having observed countless professionals struggle with manufactured online personas while others naturally developed a powerful digital presence, I've recognized that the most effective digital brands emerge through consistent relationship behaviors rather than strategic identity management.

Reputation building through thoughtful interaction with others' content creates a more authentic digital presence than self-focused broadcasting. Consistently providing insightful comments, asking thoughtful questions, and sharing valuable perspectives within community discussions establishes expertise and character more effectively than promotional content about your own accomplishments. This engagement-based reputation development creates natural recognition through demonstrated rather than claimed value.

Value creation recognition through consistent helpful contributions establishes professional identity more effectively than self-description. Regularly sharing useful resources, solving common problems, and providing genuinely beneficial information creates a reputation based on actual value delivery rather than asserted capabilities. This reliable contribution becomes associated with your digital identity, creating natural brand development through experienced rather than claimed value.

> **CONNECTION GEM:** *The most effective digital personal brands emerge from consistent relationship behaviors rather than deliberate image management. Focus on how people experience interacting with you rather than how you present yourself.*

Relationship approach characterization through distinctive interaction patterns establishes a recognizable professional identity. Consistent thoughtfulness, reliable follow-through, and generous value-sharing create distinctive relationship experiences that become associated with your digital presence. These behavioral patterns establish professional reputation through experienced interaction rather than crafted descriptions.

Community contribution reputation through meaningful participation in group discussions and challenges establishes presence through actual value rather than positioned expertise. Active engagement in solving shared problems, advancing collective understanding, and supporting community members creates recognition that emerges through demonstrated contribution rather than claimed capabilities.

Authentic rather than manufactured presence emerges through consistent behavior aligned with genuine values and capabilities. Rather than creating a strategic online persona disconnected from the actual professional approach, alignment between digital presence and authentic self creates a sustainable reputation that naturally attracts aligned opportunities. This genuine presence builds credibility through consistency rather than tactical positioning.

These relationship-based digital branding approaches create reputation through actual value delivery rather than strategic image management. By focusing on creating genuine benefit through consistent behaviors aligned with authentic capabilities, you develop a digital presence that naturally attracts appropriate opportunities without requiring manipulative impression management that characterizes much online personal branding.

Measuring Digital Networking Effectiveness

Assessing online relationship development helps refine your approach beyond simplistic metrics that often dominate digital platform evaluation. Having developed meaningful professional relationships through various online environments while observing others' fixation on vanity metrics that produce minimal valuable connections, I've identified assessment approaches that measure genuine relationship impact rather than superficial engagement statistics.

Engagement quality evaluation through depth and meaningfulness of interactions provides a more valuable assessment than simple quantity metrics. Examining whether online exchanges create substantive discussion, valuable insight sharing, and mutual benefit offers a more meaningful measurement than tracking follower counts, connection numbers, or basic engagement statistics. This qualitative assessment helps focus on relationship depth that creates actual value rather than superficial reach that generates minimal benefit.

Relationship progression tracking through natural development stages provides insight into connection effectiveness beyond initial formation. Monitoring whether digital interactions evolve from initial contact to meaningful exchange to direct communication to eventual collaboration helps evaluate whether relationships are actually developing or merely accumulating as static connections. This developmental assessment measures actual relationship value creation rather than merely connection acquisition.

> **CONNECTION GEM:** *Effective digital networking measurement focuses on relationship quality rather than vanity metrics. Connection depth, progression, and value creation matter more than follower counts or engagement statistics.*

Value creation measurement through benefits generated by digital connections provides impact assessment beyond relationship formation. Evaluating whether online relationships produce useful information sharing, valuable introductions, meaningful collaboration opportunities, or other tangible benefits helps determine whether digital networking creates actual professional value or merely relationship accumulation. This outcome-focused evaluation ensures online engagement generates meaningful results rather than simply relationship collection.

Community development assessment through the growth of a broader network ecosystem examines whether digital connections create an expanding relationship environment beyond direct interactions. Monitoring whether your online engagement facilitates connections between others, generates ongoing discussion beyond your participation, or creates self-sustaining value exchange helps evaluate the broader impact beyond immediate relationship formation. This ecosystem perspective measures network development rather than just personal connection accumulation.

Online-offline integration evaluation through successful transitions between environments measures relationship substantiveness beyond digital interaction. Tracking whether online connections develop into phone conversations, video meetings, in-person interactions, or actual collaboration helps assess whether digital relationships create comprehensive connections or remain limited to platform-based engagement. This cross-environment assessment measures relationship depth beyond purely online interaction.

These comprehensive evaluation approaches transform digital networking assessment from simplistic metric tracking to meaningful relationship development measurement. By focusing on connection quality, progression, value, ecosystem impact, and cross-environment integration rather than superficial statistics, you can accurately evaluate whether your online engagement creates valuable professional relationships or merely digital connection accumulation.

The Future of Digital Networking

Emerging technologies continuously transform connection possibilities, requiring adaptable approaches that maintain fundamental relationship principles despite changing tools. Having navigated multiple digital platform evolutions while maintaining a consistent relationship development focus, I've recognized patterns that help maintain effective connections through technological change rather than becoming distracted by tactical platform adaptation.

Core relationship values maintained despite changing tools create consistent connection effectiveness across evolving technologies. Focusing on fundamental principles—authentic engagement, genuine value creation, progressive relationship development, and long-term perspective—provides a sustainable approach regardless of specific platform features or technological capabilities. This principle-centered perspective prevents chasing tactical adaptation at the expense of meaningful relationship development.

Platform evolution preparation through understanding emerging technologies without overcommitment to specific tools maintains appropriate adaptability. Awareness of developing connection environments like immersive virtual reality, artificial intelligence matchmaking, or blockchain-based reputation systems creates appropriate understanding without premature commitment to unproven technologies. This balanced approach prevents both technological ignorance and excessive early adoption that often characterizes digital networking approaches.

> **CONNECTION GEM:** *As digital environments evolve, maintaining focus on authentic relationship principles will serve you better than chasing specific platform tactics. The technologies change constantly, but genuine connection fundamentals remain remarkably consistent.*

Understanding the possibilities of different platform types helps leverage unique capabilities while maintaining a consistent relationship approach. Recognizing how various digital environments—text-based discussion, visual platform engagement, audio conversation, and immersive interaction—create different connection possibilities allows appropriate tool selection without fundamental strategy changes. This environment-aware perspective maintains consistent relationship principles while leveraging specific technological capabilities.

Artificial intelligence relationship implications require particular consideration as recommendation algorithms, communication suggestions, and connection matchmaking increasingly influence digital interaction. Understanding how these technologies shape relationship opportunities while maintaining a human-centered connection focus creates appropriate technological leverage without surrendering authentic engagement to algorithmic direction. This balanced perspective uses AI as a relationship tool rather than a connection determinant.

Physical-digital integration navigation becomes increasingly important as the distinction between online and offline interaction continues blurring through mobile technology, augmented reality, location-aware applications, and seamless transitions between digital and physical environments. Understanding how these integrated connection contexts create comprehensive relationship opportunities rather than separate networking realms allows a unified approach that transcends the artificial online/offline division.

These forward-looking perspectives maintain an effective relationship development focus despite continuous technological evolution. By focusing on fundamental connection principles while appropriately leveraging changing tools, you create a sustainable digital networking approach that remains effective through constant technological transformation rather than requiring perpetual tactical adaptation to maintain connection effectiveness.

Chapter Takeaways

1. Digital networking requires balancing content creation, direct engagement, and community participation.
2. The most valuable online relationships typically develop gradually through authentic interaction.

3. Strategic platform selection creates a more effective presence than attempting omnipresence.
4. Value-first content catalyzes meaningful relationships without aggressive networking tactics.
5. Transitioning from digital to physical connection represents a critical relationship development point.
6. Consistency and reliability build the trust necessary for meaningful online relationship development.
7. Ethical, authentic approaches yield greater long-term digital connection value than manipulative tactics.

Action Steps

1. **Conduct a Digital Presence Audit**
    - ☐ Assess current platform effectiveness for your connection goals.
    - ☐ Evaluate content creation approach and relationship impact.
    - ☐ Analyze engagement patterns and response quality.
    - ☐ Review community participation and value creation.
    - ☐ Identify priority improvement areas.
2. **Develop Your Digital Connection Strategy**
    - ☐ Select primary relationship-building platforms.
    - ☐ Create content approach that facilitates connection.

- [ ] Build engagement strategy based on authentic interaction.
- [ ] Develop community participation framework.
- [ ] Establish online-offline integration approach.

3. **Create Your Digital Value Proposition**
    - [ ] Identify unique insights and capabilities you can share.
    - [ ] Develop content formats that showcase your perspective.
    - [ ] Build engagement approach that creates consistent benefit.
    - [ ] Create digital-specific value offerings.
    - [ ] Establish reputation development framework.

4. **Enhance Your Digital Engagement Quality**
    - [ ] Develop thoughtful response capabilities.
    - [ ] Create genuine question frameworks.
    - [ ] Build value addition strategies.
    - [ ] Establish consistent presence approach.
    - [ ] Define appropriate personal-professional balance.

5. **Build Your Digital Community Approach**
    - [ ] Identify valuable community building opportunities.
    - [ ] Create engagement facilitation strategies.
    - [ ] Develop culture-building approaches.
    - [ ] Establish consistent value provision.
    - [ ] Build relationship facilitation framework.

As you develop your digital networking capabilities, remember that the most valuable online relationships emerge from authentic engagement rather than tactical connection attempts. Focus on creating genuine value and building meaningful interactions, and your digital presence will naturally attract aligned relationships that create significant opportunity.

In the next chapter, we'll explore how faith, purpose, and connection integrate to create not just professional success but meaningful impact that transcends career advancement alone.

> **Final Connection Gem:** *In a digital landscape increasingly dominated by algorithmic matching and automated engagement, authentic human connection becomes a rare and precious commodity. The best digital networks don't feel digital at all. When you engage genuinely, provide real value, and build meaningful connections, you create a digital presence that feels human—not just algorithmic.*

CHAPTER 11

Faith, Purpose, and Connection

"The most powerful connections aren't just about professional opportunity—they're about fulfilling your deeper purpose and creating impact that extends beyond career success alone."

Throughout my career, from Wall Street trading floors to The Master Connector Agency, I've come to recognize a fundamental reality that many networking approaches overlook: the most meaningful connections emerge when we operate from a foundation of faith, purpose, and genuine service. While strategic relationship building has certainly advanced my career, the connections that have created the most significant impact—both professionally and personally—have been those aligned with my deeper calling.

Everything changed during a season of deep prayer and reflection.

I remember sitting in quiet stillness when I felt it—a divine revelation about my purpose. I wasn't just meant to "network" or "connect" for career advancement; God called me to be a bridge. A bridge between industries, between people, between opportunities that might never have crossed paths without someone willing to make the introduction.

This insight fundamentally transformed my networking approach from self-focused advancement to purpose-driven impact. Everyone would tell me for the majority of my life that I needed to start a business because I knew so many people; I never knew what that meant because I did not have a tangible product to sell. But one day, God gave me the vision to launch my agency. He said I was going to create a space where I would bring together my network of Corporate Executives, Industry Leaders, and Successful Business Owners to help them grow their network and net worth.

In this chapter, we'll explore how faith, purpose, and connection integrate to create not just professional success but meaningful impact and personal fulfillment. Whether you approach this from a specific spiritual tradition or a broader sense of purpose, you'll discover how aligning your networking with deeper values creates more powerful relationships and more significant outcomes.

Understanding the Purpose-Connection Integration

When purpose transforms connection, several profound shifts occur. Your motivation moves from self-advancement to meaningful contribution. Your interactions become more authentic rather than strategically positioned. Your impact expands beyond personal benefit. Your motivation for relationship development becomes more sustainable, and you experience deeper satisfaction from your connection activities.

I experienced this transformation when I shifted from viewing networking primarily as a career advancement tool to seeing it as an expression of my purpose to bring together people who could create meaningful impact together. Tasks that had once felt like obligatory professional activities—attending events, following up with new contacts, maintaining relationships—suddenly became expressions of my deeper calling. This alignment created both greater effectiveness and deeper fulfillment.

This purpose integration doesn't require adopting any particular spiritual framework. While my own approach is grounded in my Christian faith, I've observed similar transformations in people whose purpose emerges from diverse spiritual traditions, humanistic values, or philosophical perspectives. The key element is connecting your relationship building to something more meaningful than mere professional advancement or personal gain.

> **CONNECTION GEM:** *Purpose-driven networking isn't just morally preferable—it's practically more effective. When your connection activities align with a deeper calling, your authenticity, persistence, and impact naturally increase without requiring additional effort.*

This alignment creates several practical advantages. When you network with purpose, everything shifts:

- You're motivated by mission, not just career goals.
- Your connections feel real, not transactional.
- You're not just collecting contacts—you're creating impact. It creates more resilient relationships that withstand professional challenges because they're rooted in something deeper than transactional exchange.

Perhaps most importantly, purpose integration transforms networking from a professional obligation into a meaningful expression of your deeper values. This integration resolves the common disconnect between professional advancement and personal fulfillment, creating coherent life purpose rather than compartmentalized pursuits. The most successful and fulfilled master connectors I've known have all discovered this alignment between their connection activities and deeper calling.

My Faith Journey in Connection Building

My approach to purpose-aligned networking has evolved significantly through my spiritual journey. For years, I kept my faith and my career in separate boxes. Sundays were for God. Mondays through Fridays? That was business. I didn't realize I was leaving my deepest values out of my professional relationships. This artificial separation created an uncomfortable compartmentalization where my deepest values remained disconnected from my daily work.

The integration awakening came during a particularly challenging career period when I felt increasingly disconnected from my professional activities despite apparent success. During an extended time of prayer and reflection, I experienced what I can only describe as divine guidance about my purpose. The revelation wasn't about abandoning my professional pursuits but rather seeing them through a completely different lens—as an expression of my calling to connect different worlds and create opportunities for others.

> **CONNECTION GEM:** *Your approach to purpose-aligned networking will naturally reflect your own spiritual journey and values. The specific expression may differ based on your tradition or beliefs, but the integration of deeper purpose with connection building creates similar powerful outcomes regardless of your particular faith background.*

This awakening led me to begin seeking guidance through prayer and reflection to direct my relationship building. Rather than making networking decisions based solely on strategic professional considerations, I incorporated spiritual discernment into choices about which relationships to develop, which communities to engage with, and which initiatives to pursue. This guidance-seeking transformed my decision-making from purely strategic to purposefully aligned.

My focus gradually shifted toward how connections could help others rather than just myself. I began evaluating potential relationships not just by what they might offer me professionally but by what value they could create for everyone involved—including communities and causes beyond immediate participants. This broader perspective transformed my networking approach from self-advancement to community impact without diminishing professional effectiveness.

I also developed legacy consciousness, building relationships with multigenerational impact in mind. Rather than focusing exclusively on immediate outcomes, I began considering how connections might create value that extended beyond current circumstances to benefit future generations. This extended timeframe transformed my thinking from quarterly results to lasting impact that might continue long after my direct involvement has ended.

Throughout this evolution, I've discovered that when my connection building aligns with my faith and purpose, doors open that strategic networking alone could never access. What some might call coincidence, I recognize as divine orchestration—relationships forming at precisely the right moment to create impact beyond what I could have engineered.

CHAPTER 11: FAITH, PURPOSE, AND CONNECTION

Discovering Your Connection Purpose

Aligning networking with purpose requires clarity about your unique calling. Without this understanding, even well-intentioned connection efforts may lack the coherence and impact that purpose alignment creates. While my own discovery process involved specific spiritual practices, I've observed similar clarity emerging through various reflective approaches across different traditions and perspectives.

Your calling is hidden in what excites you. I started noticing a pattern—I felt the most alive when bringing people together. When I introduced a corporate executive to a creative entrepreneur, something inside me lit up. These moments—watching a corporate executive discover a shared passion with a community organizer or seeing an artist find unexpected collaboration with a technologist—generated a distinctive energy unlike any other professional activity. These energy patterns provided important clues about my specific connection purpose.

Understanding your most natural ways of helping others reveals similar purpose indicators. I consistently found myself spontaneously connecting people long before I recognized this as my professional calling. Even in casual conversations, I automatically thought about whom else someone should meet or what resources might help them. This natural helping orientation provided further confirmation of my connection purpose.

> **CONNECTION GEM:** *Connection purpose typically exists at the intersection of your natural gifts, what brings you joy, what the world needs, and what aligns with your deepest values. Clarity in this area transforms networking from a tactical activity to a meaningful calling.*

Considering what meaningful difference you want to make reveals additional purpose dimensions. For me, breaking down barriers between different communities and creating opportunities for people who might otherwise remain disconnected emerged as a consistent impact desire across various phases of my career. This persistent theme provided further confirmation of my specific connection calling.

Ensuring connection activities reflect your core beliefs creates essential purpose alignment. My own faith emphasizes authentic respect for each person's inherent value regardless of external status, generous service without expectation of return, and community building across traditional boundaries. These core values naturally express themselves through my approach to relationship building, creating integrity between belief and action.

Creating a clear picture of your desired long-term impact helps further refine connection purpose. My vision of building enduring bridges between different worlds that create ongoing opportunities long after my direct involvement has ended provides guidance for specific networking decisions. This long-term perspective helps evaluate immediate activities against ultimate purpose rather than short-term outcomes alone.

These reflection approaches help identify connection purposes beyond general good intentions. By recognizing specific aspects of your unique calling, you can align networking activities with deeper meaning that creates both greater impact and personal fulfillment. This alignment doesn't require adopting any particular spiritual framework but benefits from thoughtful consideration of your distinctive gifts, values, and desired contributions.

Building Faith-Aligned Connection Habits

Integrating spiritual practices with networking creates a powerful foundation for purpose-driven relationship building. While my own approach reflects specific Christian practices, I've observed similar integration across various spiritual traditions, always producing more meaningful and effective connections when thoughtfully implemented.

Before stepping into any room, I pray. I don't just ask for success—I ask for alignment. I ask, "Lord, lead me to the right conversations. Show me where I can serve. Open doors that align with my purpose." Before important relationship-building events or significant connection decisions, I take time for prayer to ensure my approach aligns with a deeper purpose rather than merely strategic considerations. This guidance-seeking transforms networking from a purely tactical activity to purposeful engagement aligned with core values.

Regularly reconnecting with your deeper "why" prevents relationship building from becoming a mechanical routine. I've established practices that consistently remind me of my connection purpose—specific readings, reflective questions, or meaningful conversations that reground me in why these activities matter beyond professional advancement. These reconnection moments maintain authentic motivation during inevitable challenging periods.

> **CONNECTION GEM:** *Regular practices that connect your networking with deeper purposes create a foundation for more meaningful relationships. These habits help maintain authentic motivation when building connections becomes challenging or results aren't immediately visible.*

Maintaining awareness of desired meaningful outcomes shapes relationship development beyond immediate transactions. By regularly considering what lasting impact I hope will emerge from connection efforts, I maintain focus on purpose rather than merely tactical networking. This outcome awareness transforms interaction from a short-term transaction to a meaningful impact opportunity without sacrificing practical effectiveness.

Acknowledging connections as gifts rather than personal achievements creates appropriate humility and gratitude. I regularly express appreciation for the relationships I've been blessed with, recognizing their development as something beyond my own strategic creation. This gratitude orientation prevents the pride and entitlement that often undermine authentic connection when networking success occurs.

Approaching relationships with a contribution mindset focused on service rather than extraction creates authentic engagement. I consistently begin interactions by considering how I might genuinely help others rather than what I might gain. This service orientation naturally expresses deeper spiritual values while creating more effective relationship development than transactional approaches.

These integrative habits maintain a connection between networking activities and deeper purpose, preventing the compartmentalization that often separates professional advancement from meaningful values. By establishing specific practices that consistently align relationship building with core purpose, you maintain authentic motivation and impact orientation regardless of changing circumstances or immediate outcomes.

The Heart Posture of Authentic Connection

Your internal orientation significantly impacts relationship quality regardless of external techniques or strategies. I've observed this reality consistently throughout my career—the most effective connectors maintain heart postures that create authentic engagement regardless of specific tactics or circumstances.

People know when you're genuinely interested. Instead of looking at someone and thinking, "How can they help me?" ask, "Who are they? What matters to them? How can I serve?" Curiosity unlocks connection. This authentic curiosity emerges from recognizing the inherent value in each person beyond their immediate utility.

Focusing on how you can contribute value transforms networking from extraction to service. When your primary internal question shifts from "What can I get from this relationship?" to "How might I genuinely help this person?", interactions naturally become more authentic and effective. This contribution orientation reflects deeper purpose while creating more powerful connections than self-focused approaches.

> **CONNECTION GEM:** *Internal orientation matters more than external techniques in building meaningful connections. People respond more to your genuine heart posture than to specific networking tactics—they sense whether you're truly interested or merely strategic.*

Combining healthy self-worth with appropriate modesty creates a balanced connection approach. Recognizing your own value without needing to prove or promote it creates a secure presence that enhances relationship quality. This balanced self-perception prevents both the insecurity and arrogance that often undermine effective connection, allowing authentic engagement from appropriate confidence.

Viewing opportunities from generosity rather than scarcity transforms competitive networking into collaborative community building. When you genuinely believe there's enough success available for everyone rather than limited resources requiring a competitive advantage, relationships develop more authentically. This abundance perspective creates a more open, generous connection that ultimately generates greater opportunity than a protective scarcity orientation.

Bringing your true self to interactions creates an authentic presence that enhances relationship quality. When you engage from your genuine identity rather than a constructed professional persona, connections develop more meaningfully and effectively. This authentic presence emerges from internal coherence between your deepest values and external expressions rather than a compartmentalized professional performance.

These heart postures create a foundation for authentic connection beyond specific techniques or strategies. While tactical approaches certainly matter, internal orientation ultimately determines relationship quality more powerfully than external methods. The most effective connectors maintain heart postures aligned with a deeper purpose, creating authentic engagement that naturally produces meaningful relationships regardless of specific networking contexts.

Purpose-Driven Relationship Selection

Meaningful impact requires discernment about which connections to develop. Without thoughtful selection, even purpose-driven networking can become scattered and ineffective despite good intentions. While my own discernment process incorporates specific spiritual guidance, I've observed similar selection wisdom emerging through various reflective approaches across different perspectives.

Assessing how a relationship serves your calling provides essential purpose alignment. I regularly consider whether potential connections align with my specific purpose of bridging different worlds and creating opportunities through relationships. This alignment evaluation ensures networking activities remain focused on meaningful impact rather than merely expanding contact lists or chasing status connections.

Ensuring basic compatibility with your core principles prevents relationship development that compromises fundamental values. I evaluate whether potential connections can proceed with mutual respect for essential ethical boundaries and human dignity requirements. This compatibility assessment maintains integrity between purpose and action rather than pursuing relationship advantage at the expense of core principles.

CHAPTER 11: FAITH, PURPOSE, AND CONNECTION

> **CONNECTION GEM:** *Not every connection is meant for you. Just because someone is powerful, influential, or well-connected doesn't mean they align with your purpose. Ask yourself: Do we share values? Does this relationship align with my calling? Will this connection lead to meaningful impact?*

Confirming potential for genuine two-way value ensures sustainable relationship development. I consider whether connections offer balanced benefit potential where both parties can authentically contribute and receive value appropriate to their needs and capabilities. This mutual benefit assessment prevents exploitative or unsustainable relationships that ultimately undermine both purpose and effectiveness.

Considering personal development potential identifies growth opportunities beyond immediate practical benefits. I evaluate whether connections might challenge my assumptions, expand my perspective, or develop my capabilities in alignment with deeper purpose. This growth consideration ensures relationship selection contributes to personal development that enhances impact capability rather than merely maintaining comfortable connection patterns.

Evaluating broader effects beyond immediate benefit assesses community impact potential. I consider how connections might create value beyond direct participants to benefit broader communities or causes aligned with deeper purpose. This extended impact evaluation ensures relationship selection contributes to meaningful change beyond personal advancement or individual benefit.

These discernment approaches ensure relationship development remains aligned with deeper purpose rather than defaulting to indiscriminate networking or purely strategic connection. By thoughtfully selecting which relationships to actively develop based on purpose alignment, you create more meaningful impact while avoiding the scattered ineffectiveness that often characterizes unfocused network building, despite good intentions.

The Entrepreneurial-Purpose Connection

Building ventures aligned with calling creates powerful integration between business development and deeper purpose. My experience with The Master Connector Agency has demonstrated how aligning entrepreneurial activities with specific purpose creates both greater impact and personal fulfillment without sacrificing professional success.

Ensuring your business serves a meaningful calling forms the foundation of purpose-aligned entrepreneurship. The Master Connector Agency emerged specifically to fulfill my purpose of bridging different worlds and creating opportunities through strategic relationship building. This direct alignment ensures business activities naturally express deeper calling rather than requiring artificial connection between separate professional and purpose pursuits.

Building core principles into an operational foundation establishes purpose integrity throughout the business. I've incorporated values like authentic respect for all participants regardless of status, genuine service orientation beyond transactions, and community benefit beyond client outcomes directly into business operations. This structural integration ensures purpose expression through everyday activities rather than remaining an abstract aspiration.

> **CONNECTION GEM:** *Purpose-aligned entrepreneurship creates uniquely integrated impact opportunities. Building ventures that serve a calling while creating sustainable value offers a powerful platform for meaningful contribution.*

Tracking meaningful differences alongside profits creates comprehensive success measurement. Beyond standard business metrics, I regularly assess relationship quality, community impact, and purpose alignment outcomes from our activities. This balanced evaluation ensures business success includes purpose fulfillment rather than merely financial performance, despite mission statements to the contrary.

Creating appropriate financial and purpose equilibrium maintains sustainable impact capability. I've established business models that generate sufficient financial returns to sustain operations while ensuring service delivery remains aligned with deeper purpose rather than compromised by profit maximization. This balanced approach prevents both the unsustainable idealism of purpose without viability and purpose compromise for financial gain.

Building an organization that serves a broader ecosystem creates extended impact beyond immediate business outcomes. I've structured Master Connector initiatives to strengthen connections between different communities, enhance capability development beyond direct clients, and create ongoing relationship infrastructure that continues generating value beyond specific engagements. This ecosystem approach extends purpose impact beyond transactions to create lasting community benefit.

These integration approaches prevent the common purpose-profit dichotomy that forces a choice between meaningful contribution and professional success. By thoughtfully aligning entrepreneurial activities with a specific calling, you create ventures that naturally express deeper purpose through everyday operations while generating sustainable value that enables ongoing impact rather than requiring separate personal and professional pursuits.

Navigating Different Belief Systems

Creating purpose-aligned connections across various traditions requires specific approaches that respect different perspectives while maintaining authentic engagement. Having built relationships across diverse spiritual and philosophical backgrounds throughout my career, I've developed approaches that create meaningful connections without requiring shared belief systems.

Identifying shared values across traditions builds connection foundations beyond specific theological frameworks. Despite different religious or philosophical perspectives, I consistently find common ground in values like human dignity, authentic respect, genuine service, and community benefit. These shared commitments create meaningful connections despite theological differences that might otherwise create barriers.

Showing genuine appreciation for different perspectives creates authentic engagement across traditions. Rather than merely tolerating different viewpoints as necessary accommodations, I approach diverse perspectives with genuine interest and respect that recognize potential wisdom beyond my own tradition. This authentic appreciation builds trust that enables meaningful connections despite different belief frameworks.

> **CONNECTION GEM:** *Faith may look different from person to person—but love, integrity, and purpose transcend belief systems. We may not always pray the same way or use the same words, but respect, authenticity, and generosity build bridges. Authentic respect for different perspectives creates relationship foundations despite diverse spiritual traditions.*

Using appropriate terminology for various contexts demonstrates respectful engagement that enhances cross-tradition connections. I adapt language to different environments without compromising core values or authentic expression, using terms and concepts that resonate within specific contexts rather than imposing terminology from my own tradition. This communication sensitivity creates comfortable engagement without requiring artificial neutrality.

Bringing your values while honoring others' creates authentic connections without imposing perspectives. I engage from my own authentic values while respecting others' right to different viewpoints, creating space for genuine dialogue without demanding agreement. This balanced approach allows meaningful relationships despite different belief systems rather than requiring artificial consensus or suppressed differences.

Focusing on mutual service opportunities creates practical collaboration beyond philosophical differences. I emphasize shared practical goals that align with different value systems rather than requiring agreement on underlying philosophical frameworks. This practical orientation creates meaningful cooperation despite different belief systems that might otherwise prevent valuable collaboration.

These navigation approaches transform potential barriers into opportunities for authentic connection across diverse traditions and perspectives. By focusing on shared values, demonstrating genuine respect, and emphasizing practical collaboration rather than philosophical agreement, you create meaningful relationships across different belief systems without requiring artificial neutrality or compromised authenticity.

CHAPTER 11: FAITH, PURPOSE, AND CONNECTION

The Calling Discernment Process

Identifying authentic connection purposes requires ongoing reflection, as purposes often emerge progressively rather than through single revelations. While my own discernment process incorporates specific spiritual practices, I've observed similar clarity developing through various reflective approaches across different traditions and perspectives.

Exploring what genuinely energizes you reveals important purpose indicators beyond strategic consideration. I regularly reflect on which connection activities create deep engagement and fulfillment rather than merely professional advancement or obligation fulfillment. These energy patterns provide crucial clues about authentic calling beyond rational analysis of career advantages.

Identifying your natural abilities and talents highlights potential purpose dimensions aligned with innate strengths. I've discovered that my natural pattern recognition across different contexts, comfort connecting with diverse people, and ability to translate between different perspectives all indicate purpose alignment with bridge-building activities. These natural capabilities often reveal calling elements more clearly than abstract consideration alone.

> **CONNECTION GEM:** *Connection purpose typically emerges at the intersection of multiple elements rather than through a single revelation. Ongoing reflection across these different aspects helps clarify authentic calling that can guide networking activities.*

Understanding what your community genuinely requires identifies meaningful contribution opportunities beyond personal preference. I regularly consider what specific needs exist within my professional and geographical communities that might align with my particular capabilities and values. These community needs provide external validation of purpose directions beyond subjective inclination.

Clarifying what meaningful difference you want to make ensures purpose alignment with deeper values rather than merely strategic positioning. I periodically revisit what specific impact I want my connection activities to create beyond career advancement or professional recognition. This impact consideration maintains purpose integrity rather than allowing gradual drift toward self-advancement despite purpose language.

Looking for external validation of an internal sense creates balanced discernment beyond purely subjective impression. I attend to feedback from trusted advisors, observable impact patterns, and community responses to different connection activities alongside internal reflection. This integrated assessment prevents both ignoring external wisdom and abandoning authentic purpose for others' expectations.

These discernment approaches create ongoing clarity about connection purpose through progressive reflection rather than expecting a single definitive revelation. By regularly considering these different dimensions, you develop an increasingly clear understanding of your authentic calling that can guide networking activities toward meaningful impact rather than merely strategic advancement despite purpose language.

Chapter Takeaways

1. Purpose-driven networking creates deeper motivation and more meaningful outcomes.
2. Your unique connection calling emerges at the intersection of gifts, passions, and needs.
3. Internal heart posture matters more than external techniques for authentic relationships.
4. Thoughtful discernment about which connections to develop ensures alignment with purpose.
5. Entrepreneurial ventures can express a deeper calling through aligned business activities.
6. Connection across different belief systems becomes possible through a shared values focus.

Action Steps

1. **Clarify Your Connection Purpose**
    - ☐ Identify patterns in what energizes and fulfills you.
    - ☐ Consider your natural contribution methods.
    - ☐ Reflect on the meaningful difference you want to make.

- [ ] Ensure alignment with core values.
- [ ] Create a clear vision for the desired long-term impact.

2. **Develop Your Faith-Connection Integration**
   - [ ] Create guidance-seeking practices for networking.
   - [ ] Build purpose reminders into connection activities.
   - [ ] Develop an impact focus for relationship building.
   - [ ] Establish gratitude practices for networking.
   - [ ] Build a service orientation for connections.

3. **Create Your Heart Posture Foundation**
   - [ ] Develop genuine interest cultivation practices.
   - [ ] Build a service mindset for relationships.
   - [ ] Create an appropriate humility balance.
   - [ ] Establish an abundance perspective.
   - [ ] Strengthen your authenticity commitment.

4. **Build Your Stewardship Approach**
   - [ ] Develop gift recognition for relationships.
   - [ ] Create connection development practices.
   - [ ] Build an impact orientation for networking.
   - [ ] Establish legacy consideration.
   - [ ] Strengthen your gratitude foundation.

5. **Enhance Your Bridge-Building Service**
   - ☐ Identify gaps you're uniquely positioned to address.
   - ☐ Develop translation capabilities for different groups.
   - ☐ Create connection facilitation approaches.
   - ☐ Build value demonstration capabilities.
   - ☐ Establish sustainability development strategies.

As you develop your purpose-aligned connection approach, remember that the most meaningful networking isn't just about career advancement but about fulfilling your deeper calling. When your relationship building aligns with your core values and serves a purpose beyond self-interest, both professional success and personal fulfillment naturally follow.

In the next chapter, we'll explore the ripple effect of connection—how your networking creates an impact that extends far beyond your direct relationships, creating a legacy that continues generating value for generations to come.

Final Connection Gem: *In a world increasingly focused on metrics and tactics, purpose-driven networking creates distinctive value that technical approaches alone cannot achieve. You were never meant to network just for yourself. When you align your connections with your faith and purpose, you create something bigger than business. You build legacy. And legacy doesn't just build careers—it changes lives.*

CHAPTER 12

The Ripple Effect: Creating a Connection Legacy

"The true measure of your connection mastery isn't just the opportunities it creates for you, but the impact it generates for others far beyond your direct relationships."

The email arrived unexpectedly: "Nichole, I need to tell you something important. Five years ago, you introduced me to someone who changed my career trajectory. That connection led to an opportunity that allowed me to mentor three young professionals who have now started their own businesses. Today, one of those companies just hired ten people from our community. I'm sitting here realizing that none of this would have happened without that single introduction you made. Your ripple effect is changing lives you've never even met."

This message captures what I consider the ultimate reward of connection mastery—the exponential impact that extends far beyond your direct relationships. Throughout my career, I've discovered that the most meaningful networking isn't measured by the opportunities it creates for you personally, but by the cascading effect it generates through others.

When I first entered Wall Street as an equity trader, my networking was primarily focused on my own advancement. But as my career progressed, I began to recognize the extraordinary power of deliberately creating ripple effects—intentionally connecting people, sharing opportunities, and building systems that generated impact extending far beyond my immediate circle.

From introducing community leaders to corporate executives, connecting entrepreneurs with investors, mentoring young professionals, or creating programs that established entirely new relationship ecosystems, I've witnessed how strategic connections can create waves of impact that continue generating value long after my direct involvement has ended.

In this chapter, we'll explore how to maximize your connection ripple effect—how to create a networking impact that extends beyond your immediate relationships to touch lives you'll never directly meet. You'll discover how paying forward the benefits you've received not only creates a meaningful legacy but actually enhances your own network value in the process.

Chapter 12: The Ripple Effect: Creating a Connection Legacy

Understanding the Connection Ripple Effect

Every meaningful connection you make has the potential to multiply far beyond what you can see. Think about it: When you introduce two people, they each have their own circles of influence. One introduction can lead to dozens, hundreds, even thousands of new opportunities across generations.

Here's how the ripple effect works:

1. Exponential growth: A single introduction can lead to multiple additional relationships.
2. Knowledge transfer: When ideas and insights spread beyond the initial connection, entire industries and communities benefit.
3. Opportunity multiplication: The right connection can lead to new jobs, business partnerships, and life-changing mentorships.
4. Resource amplification: People bring skills, funding, and expertise that create opportunities beyond what one person could provide alone.
5. Legacy impact: The ripple effect continues long after your direct involvement, shaping lives you may never meet.

A single thoughtful introduction between two people might lead each of them to introduce others, creating an ever-widening circle of impact beginning from that initial connection.

Knowledge transfer occurs as information and insights flow through extended networks, creating impact far beyond initial sharing. When I connect a corporate executive with community leaders, the insights they exchange often spread throughout their respective organizations, influencing decisions and approaches far beyond their direct conversation. This knowledge expansion creates impact that extends far beyond the original relationship.

Opportunity multiplication happens as possibilities expand across connection chains. When I introduced a promising entrepreneur to an investor who funded her venture, that business created employment opportunities for dozens of people who never met either me or the investor. These extended opportunity chains generate an impact that's impossible to create through direct effort alone, regardless of individual capability or resources.

> **CONNECTION GEM:** *The mathematics of ripple effects create extraordinary multiplication potential. While you might directly know hundreds of people, your second-degree connections (friends of friends) likely number in the tens of thousands, with third-degree connections potentially reaching millions.*

Resource amplification occurs when capabilities combine in unexpected ways across network levels. A technology expert I connected with a community organization later brought in additional colleagues who volunteered specialized skills that the organization could never have afforded. These resource synergies throughout extended networks create an impact far exceeding what any direct contribution could achieve, regardless of individual generosity.

Impact longevity increases as effects continue generating value over extended time periods. Connections I facilitated between corporate and educational institutions years ago continue producing ongoing benefits for students who weren't even born when those relationships formed. This temporal extension creates a compounding impact impossible through isolated current efforts, regardless of their immediate effectiveness.

These multiplication mechanisms transform individual networking from limited personal interaction to potentially limitless impact expansion. By understanding how connection ripples extend through relationships, knowledge, opportunities, resources, and time, you shift focus from maximizing personal network value to creating strategic impact that continues expanding far beyond your direct involvement.

My Ripple Effect Journey

I didn't always think this way. When I started my career as an equity trader on Wall Street, networking was purely a strategy for personal advancement. I was focused on whom I could meet, what doors I could open, and how fast I could climb.

But something changed.

As I moved through my career, I started noticing the ripple effects of my introductions. I saw mentees land life-changing opportunities, businesses form through a single handshake, and entire communities impacted because of one thoughtful connection.

That's when I realized: my legacy wouldn't be about how many doors I walked through—it would be about how many doors I helped others open.

This evolution began with a self-focused phase when I initially concentrated on personal advancement opportunities. My early trading career networking aimed primarily at building relationships that would help me progress professionally, with minimal consideration for broader impact beyond my own success.

This limited perspective gradually transformed through direct impact recognition as I observed how connections benefited immediate relationships beyond myself. Watching the mutual value created when I introduced people who could help each other—even when I received no direct benefit—began expanding my understanding of connection value beyond personal advantage. This widening perspective initiated my evolution toward more purposeful network development.

System awareness development marked a crucial advancement as I began to understand broader network effects beyond direct relationships. Recognizing how connections created ripples throughout extended relationship systems—affecting people two, three, or more degrees removed from the initial introduction—dramatically expanded my perception of networking impact. This understanding of systems transformed my approach from creating individual connections to developing impact-focused relationship ecosystems.

> **CONNECTION GEM:** *Your approach to impact creation should evolve from immediate benefits to systematic ripple effects. The most powerful connection legacy typically emerges from deliberate ecosystem building rather than isolated relationship development.*

Intentional ripple creation followed as I deliberately fostered specific impact types that extended beyond direct relationships. Rather than just making beneficial introductions as opportunities arose, I began strategically identifying connection gaps and building bridges specifically to generate extended impact. This proactive approach transformed networking from reactive opportunity response to deliberate impact design through thoughtful relationship engineering.

Legacy building represents my current focus—creating sustainable systems for ongoing effect generation beyond my direct involvement. My work establishing connection communities, developing relationship infrastructures, and creating self-sustaining networking methodologies aims to produce impact that continues long after my personal participation. This legacy orientation transforms networking from a temporary personal activity to an enduring impact mechanism that benefits generations beyond my own.

Throughout this evolution, I've discovered that the most powerful ripple effects typically emerge from relationships built with a genuine service orientation rather than strategic networking alone. The most meaningful impact often comes through connections created with generous intent rather than calculated advancement, even when that generosity extends far beyond direct recipients to people you'll never personally meet.

System Building for Extended Impact

If you want to build a lasting ripple effect, you can't rely on one-time connections. The key to exponential impact is building systems—creating platforms, communities, and frameworks that allow relationships to thrive without your constant involvement.

Here's how to build connection ecosystems that multiply impact:

- Community Development: Foster spaces (online or in-person) where people consistently connect and grow.
- Platforms & Programs: Create systems that allow networking to happen without your direct involvement (mentorship programs, online groups, recurring events).
- Cultural Impact: Establish norms and values that shape relationships long after you're gone.

CHAPTER 12: THE RIPPLE EFFECT: CREATING A CONNECTION LEGACY

When you create a system, you don't just build connections—you build a movement.

This system-building approach has proven to be the most powerful method for creating impact that continues expanding without requiring your direct involvement in every relationship formed.

Community development represents the foundation of extended impact creation. By establishing environments where people regularly connect around shared purposes, interests, or goals, you create self-sustaining relationship ecosystems that continue generating value beyond your facilitation. My quarterly cross-industry dinners evolved from events I personally orchestrated into self-sustaining communities where participants independently develop relationships that create ongoing impact without my direct involvement in every connection formed.

Platform creation develops environments for continuous connection beyond your personal introductions. Building structured frameworks—whether online communities, regular gathering formats, or relationship methodologies—creates mechanisms for ongoing connection that don't require your facilitation for every relationship developed. These platforms transform individual networking capacity into exponentially expanded impact potential through systematic relationship formation beyond your direct involvement.

> **CONNECTION GEM:** *System building creates some of the most powerful and enduring ripple effects because it establishes self-sustaining impact environments. Creating platforms and communities often generates influence that continues long after your direct involvement ends.*

Program establishment creates structured impact initiatives that systematically address connection needs beyond individual introductions. Developing organized approaches—like the mentorship programs I've created that connect experienced professionals with emerging leaders—creates systematic relationship building that addresses consistent connection patterns rather than requiring unique solutions for each situation. These programs transform individual networking effectiveness into institutional impact mechanisms that generate ongoing value beyond personal capacity.

Culture formation develops values and norms that shape interaction beyond your direct participation. Establishing explicit principles, behavioral expectations, and relational approaches within communities creates consistent connection quality without requiring your presence in every interaction. These cultural foundations transform individual relationship influence into community impact standards that maintain quality as networks expand beyond your direct involvement.

Infrastructure building constructs supporting elements for relationship development beyond your facilitation. Creating tools, resources, and processes that help others build meaningful connections independently extends your impact far beyond personal capacity limitations. These supporting mechanisms transform individual connection capability into expanded community impact through enhanced collective relationship development capacity.

These system approaches represent the highest leverage connection strategies because they create environments where relationship impact continuously multiplies without requiring your direct involvement in every connection formed. By establishing these self-sustaining ecosystems, your networking influence extends far beyond personal capacity limitations to create a lasting legacy that continues benefiting people you'll never directly meet.

Generational Impact Development

Your connections don't just impact today; they shape entire generations.

Imagine a young entrepreneur you mentor today. In ten years, they become a CEO, hiring dozens of employees and mentoring others. Those mentees start their own businesses, each impacting hundreds more. This is legacy.

Here's how to build generational impact:

- Mentorship: Invest in people who will go on to create their own ripple effects.

- Knowledge Transfer: Share your insights in ways that will last—books, videos, courses, mentorship programs.
- Value Transmission: Teach principles, not just tactics—kindness, generosity, and integrity.

The best leaders don't just build careers. They build legacies.

This temporal extension transforms networking from creating an immediate impact to establishing enduring value that continues long after your direct involvement has ended.

Mentorship investment develops next-generation talent and leadership through structured guidance relationships. By thoughtfully connecting with emerging professionals to share knowledge, perspective, and opportunity, you create an impact that extends throughout their careers and influences everyone they subsequently affect. The young professionals I've mentored now lead organizations, influence industries, and mentor others themselves—creating cascading impact that will continue for generations beyond my original investment.

Knowledge transfer ensures critical insights continue beyond your direct sharing through deliberate documentation and transmission. By creating frameworks, methodologies, and resources that capture your connection approaches, you enable others to implement similar impact strategies without requiring your direct guidance. These knowledge resources transform temporary personal wisdom into enduring community assets that continue creating value long after your direct participation ends.

> **CONNECTION GEM:** *Generational impact represents one of the most meaningful ripple effect dimensions. Deliberately developing connections with a multi-generational perspective significantly enhances your legacy beyond immediate influence.*

Value transmission passes core principles to future impact creators through explicit articulation and demonstration. By clearly communicating the fundamental values underlying effective connection—authentic engagement, genuine service, trust building, long-term perspective—you create a philosophical foundation that shapes how subsequent generations approach relationship building. This values-based guidance transforms temporary behavioral influence into enduring philosophical impact that shapes future connection approaches.

Opportunity structure building creates sustainable access pathways that remain available beyond your direct provision. By establishing programs, platforms, and processes that systematically create opportunity access for underrepresented groups, you build mechanisms that continue generating equitable possibilities long after your direct involvement. These enduring structures transform temporary personal opportunity sharing into institutional impact mechanisms that benefit generations beyond immediate recipients.

Leadership development invests in future ripple effect generators through deliberate capability building. By identifying and cultivating connection-oriented leaders who will create their own relationship impact, you establish succession that continues meaningful networking approaches beyond your direct participation. This leadership pipeline transforms individual connection mastery into multigenerational impact through sustained implementation of effective relationship approaches.

These generational approaches extend your connection impact far beyond immediate temporal limitations. By deliberately developing relationships, systems, and capabilities with a multi-generational perspective, you create a legacy that continues to benefit people long after your direct involvement has ended—transforming temporary personal networking into enduring community impact that spans generations.

Technology for Ripple Amplification

Technology, when used strategically, has the power to magnify your connections and extend your impact beyond physical limitations. While nothing can replace the human-to-human element of authentic networking, digital tools serve as force multipliers, allowing you to expand reach, share knowledge, and sustain influence in ways that traditional networking alone cannot achieve.

Technology eliminates distance as a limiting factor. Through online platforms, communities, and social networks, you can

CHAPTER 12: THE RIPPLE EFFECT: CREATING A CONNECTION LEGACY

build relationships across cities, countries, and industries—introducing people who may never have crossed paths otherwise. My online communities connect professionals across continents who subsequently develop valuable relationships without requiring my physical presence in their locations. This geographic expansion transforms regionally limited networking into global impact potential through extended connection reach.

What once had to be shared in one-on-one meetings can now be broadcast to thousands through webinars, podcasts, blogs, and digital resources. This ability to distribute valuable insights at scale accelerates the ripple effect of knowledge sharing far beyond your immediate circle. These distribution mechanisms transform limited personal knowledge sharing into exponentially expanded impact through scalable information provision without requiring individual interaction with every recipient.

> **CONNECTION GEM:** *Technology dramatically enhances ripple effect potential through geographic boundary elimination and scale creation. Strategic digital tool utilization can significantly amplify your connection impact beyond what would be possible through traditional relationship building alone.*

One of the most powerful ways to create a lasting impact is by building online communities where relationships form organically. Virtual masterminds, LinkedIn groups, private membership forums, and digital networking events create self-sustaining relationship hubs, ensuring that valuable connections continue even when you're not directly involved.

Digital communities create relationship infrastructure supporting thousands of connections that would be logistically impossible through purely in-person approaches. These expanded environments transform limited physical networking capacity into dramatically enhanced impact scale through extended participation possibilities.

Before digital networking, making an introduction required phone calls, handwritten letters, or scheduling in-person meetings. Now, a single LinkedIn message, email, or video introduction can seamlessly connect two people across time zones in seconds.

Digital tools enable relationship initiation across distances, time zones, and contextual barriers that would create prohibitive logistical challenges through purely physical approaches. These facilitation mechanisms transform limited personal introduction capacity into expanded connection capability through enhanced coordination efficiency.

One of the greatest challenges of networking is not always seeing the full extent of your impact. However, digital tools like analytics, network mapping, and engagement tracking help provide visibility into how connections evolve over time.

Analytics, network mapping, and relationship visualization technologies reveal connection impacts occurring beyond personal perception limitations, providing insights that improve strategic impact development. These tracking capabilities transform limited anecdotal understanding into comprehensive ripple awareness through enhanced visibility beyond direct relationship observation.

These technological approaches dramatically enhance ripple effect development beyond what purely physical networking could achieve. By strategically leveraging digital tools while maintaining an authentic relationship foundation, you create expanded impact through enhanced reach, efficiency, and understanding without sacrificing the connection quality essential for meaningful ripple development.

Ripple Effect Through Mentorship

Developing others creates particularly powerful generational impact through capability enhancement that enables extended effect creation. This mentorship dimension creates distinctive ripple patterns through deliberate investment in people who subsequently generate their own expanding impact circles.

Knowledge transfer shares crucial insights and wisdom that enable others to implement effective connection approaches independently. By providing an understanding of networking principles, relationship development approaches, and strategic connection tactics, you equip mentees with capabilities that benefit everyone they subsequently interact with throughout their careers. This knowledge-sharing transforms limited personal impact into expanded influence through enhanced capability distribution across extended networks.

Skill development builds specific capabilities that enable others to create their own effective connections. By helping mentees develop relationship initiation approaches, trust-building methods, value demonstration tactics, and other practical networking abilities, you establish impact expansion mechanisms through enhanced capability replication. These skill investments transform limited personal networking effectiveness into multiplied impact through expanded implementation capacity across numerous practitioners.

> **CONNECTION GEM:** *Mentorship creates especially meaningful ripple effects through capability development that enables others' success. The skills and knowledge you help develop often create an impact extending far beyond your direct relationship with the mentee.*

Connection introduction provides access to valuable relationships that expand mentees' opportunity and impact potential. By thoughtfully connecting mentees with appropriate people in your network based on aligned interests, compatible needs, and complementary capabilities, you create a relationship foundation for their subsequent success. These introductions transform limited personal network value into expanded opportunity through strategic relationship sharing that enables mentees' advancement.

Guidance provision offers navigation support for challenges that might otherwise limit others' development and impact potential. By helping mentees address specific relationship difficulties, networking obstacles, or connection strategy questions based on your experience, you prevent limitations that would restrict their impact capacity. This guidance transforms potential development barriers into enhanced capability through experiential wisdom sharing that improves mentees' effectiveness.

Confidence building develops others' belief in their potential, which enables action beyond perceived limitations. By providing appropriate encouragement, acknowledging genuine capabilities, and creating progressive success experiences, you establish a psychological foundation for expanded impact creation through enhanced self-efficacy. This confidence development transforms potential capability restriction into expanded action through psychological barrier removal that enables fuller expression of mentees' natural abilities.

These mentorship dimensions create particularly powerful ripple effects through capability enhancement that enables others to generate their own expanding impact circles. By thoughtfully developing people who subsequently develop others, you create exponential influence expansion that continues multiplying long after your direct involvement has ended, touching countless lives beyond your personal reach or awareness.

Building Connection Wealth for Future Generations

Strategic relationship development creates enduring assets that benefit not just you but future generations through thoughtful network building with a legacy perspective. This approach transforms networking from creating immediate personal advantage to establishing enduring relationship capital that continues generating value across generations.

Knowledge wealth establishment builds information assets that retain value beyond immediate application. By documenting effective connection approaches, capturing relationship insights, and creating methodologies that others can implement independently, you develop intellectual capital that benefits future generations without requiring your direct instruction. These knowledge resources transform temporary personal understanding into enduring informational assets that continue creating value long after your direct participation ends.

Relationship infrastructure creation develops connection systems that remain valuable beyond individual interactions. By establishing communities, platforms, and programs that systematically facilitate beneficial relationships, you build relationship architecture that continues functioning independently of your personal participation. These infrastructures transform temporary personal networking into enduring connection mechanisms that benefit generations beyond your direct involvement.

> **CONNECTION GEM:** *Thoughtfully developed connection assets create some of the most valuable generational wealth because they continue generating opportunities across multiple generations. While financial capital provides an important foundation, relationship wealth often creates a more enduring advantage through sustained access to opportunities.*

Access pathway establishment creates opportunity routes that remain available to future generations. By building bridges between different communities, developing entry points to valuable networks, and creating connection patterns that others can follow, you establish access mechanisms that continue functioning beyond your personal facilitation. These pathways transform temporary personal opportunity sharing into enduring access structures that benefit generations beyond your direct provision.

Value system transmission conveys connection principles that guide effective relationship building across generations. By explicitly articulating and demonstrating core values like authentic engagement, genuine service, trust building, and reciprocal value creation, you establish a philosophical foundation that shapes how subsequent generations approach networking. This value transmission transforms temporary behavioral influence into enduring philosophical impact that guides future relationship development approaches.

Capability development creates skills in others that generate ongoing value through enhanced ability utilization. By helping people develop effective connection capabilities that they subsequently teach others, you establish continuous skill transmission that creates expanding impact across generations. This capability building transforms temporary personal effectiveness into enduring community capacity through sustained implementation capability beyond your direct participation.

These wealth-building approaches transform networking from creating temporary personal advantage to establishing enduring relationship capital that continues generating value across generations. By thoughtfully developing connection assets with a legacy perspective, you create true relationship wealth that benefits not just yourself but creates enduring advantage for future generations in more meaningful ways than purely financial inheritance could provide.

The Ultimate Purpose of Your Network

Beyond personal advancement, strategic relationships create a foundation for meaningful contribution through expanded positive impact capability. This purpose perspective transforms networking from a self-focused career advancement tool to a

CHAPTER 12: THE RIPPLE EFFECT: CREATING A CONNECTION LEGACY

community impact mechanism with significant meaning beyond professional success alone.

Opportunity multiplication for others represents one of the most meaningful network purposes beyond personal advancement. By deliberately creating connections that generate possibilities for people beyond yourself—particularly those with limited access to traditional opportunity structures—you leverage relationship capital for significant positive impact. This opportunity sharing transforms networking from an advancement mechanism to an impact creation tool through extended benefit provision beyond yourself.

Resource amplification through strategic relationship development creates expanded capability for addressing important needs. By connecting people with complementary resources—whether knowledge, skills, access, or tangible assets—you create synergies that generate enhanced problem-solving capability through collaborative application. This resource integration transforms individual contribution capacity into amplified impact potential through strategic relationship combinations that address larger challenges than individual effort could affect.

> **CONNECTION GEM:** *The most meaningful network purpose extends far beyond personal advancement to create a positive impact for others. When you leverage relationships to generate opportunities for people beyond yourself, networking transforms from a career tool to a legacy creation mechanism.*

Innovation facilitation through diverse perspective integration creates novel solutions beyond conventional approaches. By connecting people with different backgrounds, experiences, and viewpoints around common challenges, you generate creative problem-solving capabilities beyond homogeneous group limitations. This diversity leverage transforms restricted perspectives within single communities into enhanced solution development through expanded viewpoint integration across different worlds.

Support provision creates resources for others facing significant challenges beyond individual capacity. By mobilizing network assistance for people experiencing difficulties—whether professional obstacles, personal challenges, or community problems—you create enhanced resilience beyond isolated capability. This support mobilization transforms individual limitation into community resources through relationship activation that addresses needs beyond what isolated effort could accomplish.

Legacy establishment develops lasting impact beyond temporary professional success. By creating relationships, systems, and resources that continue generating value long after your direct involvement, you establish enduring positive influence that transcends career achievement. This legacy focus transforms temporary professional networking into meaningful contribution with significance extending beyond personal accomplishment to community benefit spanning generations.

These purpose dimensions transform networking from a self-advancement mechanism to a meaningful contribution tool with significance beyond career success. By focusing on how your relationships can create a positive impact for others rather than just a professional advantage for yourself, you develop a network purpose with deeper meaning and a more significant legacy than personal achievement alone could provide—regardless of how impressive those accomplishments might appear.

Chapter Takeaways

1. Connection impact extends exponentially beyond direct relationships through ripple effects.
2. Strategic introductions create particularly visible and immediate extended impact.
3. System building establishes self-sustaining environments for ongoing relationship formation.
4. Mentorship creates uniquely powerful ripples through capability multiplication.
5. Teaching connection skills generates particularly expansive impact through knowledge transfer.
6. Generational perspective builds relationship wealth that benefits future generations.
7. Creating ripples enhances your own success while generating a meaningful legacy.

Action Steps

1. **Develop Your Ripple Effect Strategy**
   - ☐ Identify specific types of impact you want to create.
   - ☐ Determine primary ripple effect approaches you'll utilize.
   - ☐ Create an intentional introduction framework.
   - ☐ Build a knowledge sharing system.
   - ☐ Develop a relationship environment approach.

2. **Enhance Your Introduction Impact**
   - ☐ Create a need-resource matching system.
   - ☐ Develop a complementary capability connection approach.
   - ☐ Build a cross-boundary introduction strategy.
   - ☐ Establish opportunity access facilitation.
   - ☐ Create a support network connection approach.

3. **Build Your Knowledge Sharing System**
   - ☐ Identify your most valuable expertise areas.
   - ☐ Create effective information sharing approaches.
   - ☐ Develop a connection education framework.
   - ☐ Build a success pattern highlighting strategy.
   - ☐ Establish challenge navigation guidance.

4. **Develop Your System Building Approach**
   - ☐ Create a community development strategy.
   - ☐ Build a platform creation framework.
   - ☐ Develop a program establishment approach.
   - ☐ Create a culture formation strategy.
   - ☐ Establish infrastructure building elements.

5. **Enhance Your Generational Impact**
   - ☐ Develop a mentorship investment approach.
   - ☐ Create a knowledge transfer system.
   - ☐ Build a value transmission strategy.
   - ☐ Develop an opportunity structure approach.
   - ☐ Establish a leadership development framework.

As you develop your ripple effect capabilities, remember that the most meaningful connection impact often emerges far beyond your direct relationships. Focus on creating not just personal opportunities but extended influence that continues generating value long after your involvement ends.

In conclusion, we'll explore how to integrate all these principles into your ongoing connection journey—creating a comprehensive approach that transforms networking from isolated tactics into cohesive relationship mastery.

Final Connection Gem: *In a world increasingly focused on immediate results and personal advancement, the ability to create powerful ripple effects becomes increasingly rare and valuable. The most valuable thing you can do isn't just to build your own success—it's to create success for others. The relationships you build today will shape communities, industries, and generations to come. Be intentional. Make the introduction. Open the door. Because you never know—one connection might just change the world. Your ripple effect isn't just the lives you touch directly—it's the lives touched because of you.*

FINAL THOUGHTS

Your Connection Journey Begins

As this book comes to a close, your journey as a connector is just beginning. We've explored the transformative power of relationships, from leading with value to building a network that creates impact beyond your direct reach. But knowledge alone isn't enough—true mastery comes from application and integration. Now, it's time to take these principles and make them part of your everyday approach to connection.

Integrating the Principles

Mastering connection isn't about using a few networking tricks—it's about adopting a holistic approach that transforms how you engage with others. Each of the 11 principles we've explored is a building block, working together to create a foundation for authentic, meaningful relationships:

1. **Leading with value** establishes the fundamental approach of focusing first on what you can contribute rather than what you can gain. This mindset shift immediately sets you apart from the 90% of networkers who lead with requests rather than contributions.
2. **Consistent follow-through** transforms initial meetings into meaningful relationships. By developing systems that ensure reliable connection maintenance, you build trust and demonstrate reliability that creates lasting professional bonds.
3. **Breaking bread** creates unique opportunities for deeper connection through the simple but powerful act of sharing meals. These experiences break down barriers that might otherwise prevent authentic relationship development.
4. **Bridging different worlds** allows you to create unique value by connecting people across industries, cultures, and communities that rarely intersect. This bridge-building capability creates opportunities that would otherwise remain invisible.
5. **Investing in access** strategically positions you in environments where valuable connections naturally occur. By thoughtfully allocating resources to create a presence in high-opportunity settings, you expand your connection possibilities far beyond what effort alone could achieve.
6. **Leveraging business resource groups** accelerates your connection development within organizations, creating

relationships across departmental and hierarchical boundaries. These internal communities provide unique opportunities for visibility and relationship building.

7. **Building your personal brand through relationships** establishes a reputation based on consistent positive experiences rather than self-promotion. This authentic approach creates a brand that attracts opportunities even when you're not in the room.

8. **Converting connections to opportunities** transforms relationships into tangible value through patient, authentic development rather than premature requests. This conversion approach creates more valuable and sustainable opportunities than transactional networking.

9. **Digital age networking** extends your connection capabilities across geographic boundaries while maintaining the authenticity that creates meaningful relationships. A strategic online presence creates global connection possibilities that complement in-person networking.

10. **Faith, purpose, and connection** integrate your networking with deeper meaning, creating alignment between your relationship building and core values. This purpose integration transforms networking from career obligation to a meaningful expression of your calling.

11. **Creating ripple effects** extends your impact far beyond direct relationships, generating a legacy that continues creating value for generations. This extended influence

transforms networking from personal advancement to meaningful contribution.

When integrated, these principles create a comprehensive approach to connection that transcends traditional networking. Rather than viewing relationship building as a series of tactical activities, you develop a connection mindset that naturally expresses itself through authentic engagement with others.

The Stages of Connection Mastery

Connection mastery is a journey, not an overnight achievement. It evolves through five distinct stages, each building upon the last:

1. The Awareness Stage

Your journey begins with recognizing the true power of authentic connection. You start seeing relationships not merely as professional necessities but as the fundamental infrastructure of opportunity, success, and meaning. This awareness creates motivation to develop beyond transactional networking to meaningful connection building.

During this stage, focus on observing successful connectors, learning fundamental principles, and beginning to implement basic approaches like leading with value and consistent follow-through. Pay particular attention to the differences between transactional networkers and authentic connectors, noting how dramatically their approaches and results differ.

2. The Implementation Stage

As awareness develops into action, you begin consistently applying connection principles in everyday interactions. You develop systems for relationship maintenance, practice value-first engagement, and establish regular connection habits that build your relationship foundation.

During this stage, focus on creating consistent implementation rather than perfect execution. Establish regular connection practices—whether weekly follow-up blocks, monthly breaking-bread gatherings, or daily value-sharing habits. These repeated behaviors gradually become natural patterns rather than conscious techniques.

3. The Specialization Stage

With consistent implementation established, you begin developing your distinctive connection approach based on your unique strengths, circumstances, and purpose. You identify specific connector types that align with your natural abilities—whether bridge-builder, convener, mentor, or knowledge-sharer—and focus on developing excellence in these areas.

During this stage, concentrate on enhancing your natural connection strengths rather than attempting to master every approach. Develop signature practices that leverage your unique capabilities while creating distinctive value aligned with your specific purpose and passion.

4. The System-Building Stage

As your individual connection capabilities mature, you begin creating environments and processes that facilitate relationships beyond your direct involvement. You establish communities, develop platforms, and build systems that create connection opportunities for others through structured approaches.

During this stage, focus on creating scalable impact through environmental design rather than solely individual connections. Develop programs, communities, and methodologies that enable others to build valuable relationships through the infrastructure you establish.

5. The Legacy Stage

In the most advanced development phase, you create a sustainable connection impact that continues generating value beyond your direct participation. You mentor others in effective relationship building, document your methodologies, and establish entities that facilitate ongoing connection long after your involvement ends.

During this stage, concentrate on developing connection capabilities in others, creating sustainable systems, and establishing enduring practices that continue creating value across generations. The focus shifts from personal impact to legacy development through multiplied influence.

Throughout these stages, progress isn't strictly linear. You'll likely move back and forth between them as you develop different aspects of your connection mastery. The journey involves continuous growth rather than reaching a final destination—there will always be new relationship dimensions to explore, connection capabilities to develop, and impact opportunities to create.

Taking the First Step Toward Becoming a Master Connector

The journey of a thousand miles begins with a single step. While the comprehensive principles we've explored might seem overwhelming, remember that authentic connection begins with simple actions consistently applied. Here are specific first steps you can take to begin your journey toward connection mastery:

> **1. Conduct a personal connection audit.** Honestly assess your current relationship-building approaches, strengths, challenges, and outcomes. Consider which principles

from this book most directly address your specific growth opportunities, and prioritize implementing those first.

2. Identify your connection purpose. Reflect on how relationship building aligns with your deeper values and calling. Consider what specific impact you hope to create through your connections and how that purpose might guide your networking approach beyond mere career advancement.

3. Establish one consistent connection habit. Rather than attempting to implement everything at once, select a single practice—perhaps weekly follow-up blocks, monthly relationship-building gatherings, or daily value-sharing—and commit to implementing it consistently for at least 30 days.

4. Create your value proposition. Identify specific ways you can consistently contribute value to your connections based on your unique knowledge, experience, skills, or perspective. Develop approaches for sharing this value authentically rather than through overt self-promotion.

5. Select three connection investments. Identify specific resources—whether time, money, or energy—you'll deliberately allocate to building valuable relationships. These might include joining specific groups, attending certain events, or creating particular environments that facilitate meaningful connection.

6. Build your support system. Identify people who can encourage your connection journey, provide honest feedback, and help you implement these principles consistently. Share your goals with them and establish regular check-in points to maintain accountability and momentum.

7. Find your connection community. Seek out others committed to authentic relationship building who can provide encouragement, share experiences, and offer perspective as you develop your connection capabilities. These communities provide both support and valuable learning opportunities.

As you take these first steps, remember that connection mastery develops through consistent practice rather than perfect implementation. Every authentic interaction, thoughtful follow-up, and genuine value contribution builds your capability and reputation as a connector. Small actions consistently applied create exponentially greater impact over time than occasional grand gestures.

The world needs more master connectors—people who build authentic bridges between different communities, create opportunities for those who might otherwise remain disconnected, and generate ripple effects that benefit generations beyond their direct relationships. As you implement the principles we've explored, you become not just a more effective networker but a creator of meaningful impact through authentic connection.

Your journey toward connection mastery begins now, with your very next interaction. Will you lead with value? Will you follow through consistently? Will you approach relationships with purpose beyond personal gain? The choices you make in these moments gradually transform you from someone who simply knows people into someone who creates authentic, meaningful impact through strategic relationship building.

I invite you to embrace this journey with both strategic intention and authentic engagement. The path of the master connector isn't merely about building an impressive contact list—it's about creating meaningful impact through relationships grounded in genuine value exchange. It's about becoming someone who doesn't just collect connections but creates opportunities, builds bridges, and leaves a legacy of relationships that continue generating value long after your direct involvement has ended.

The world is waiting for the unique connections only you can create. Your journey as a master connector begins now.

Acknowledgements

First and foremost, I offer my deepest gratitude to God, who gave me the vision to create the Master Connector Agency, and whose unwavering will empowered me to write this book, dedicated to helping others master the art of connection to achieve both networking and financial success.

I want to thank Ash Cash, Nicole Queen, and the team at 1Brick Publishing for helping me produce this book in less than 30 days. I am grateful for their countless hours of helping me craft my message in the most impactful way.

I want to thank my husband for proofreading the book and providing me guidance on the most impactful stories to incorporate.

Special thanks to my friends (Candace, Naima, Nina, & Corlette) who took the time to read the book in advance and offered me their helpful feedback.

Special thanks to my friends and family who took the time to read my book and share their incredible insights and heartfelt quotes about me and my work:

Valerie Harmon-Parker (Mom)

Brian Parker (Dad)

Lydell & Brittany Dewberry (Brother & Sister-in-Law)

Brianna Parker (Sister)

Greg Pointdujour (Husband)

Zackary Simmons-Glover (Brother)

Egypt Sherrod

Yandy Smith Harris

Cynthia Bailey

Valeisha Butterfield

Ian Dunlap

Arinze Onugha, ESQ

Tiffany Cobb

Ebony Frazier

Pamela Tucker

Shannon Carter

Corlette Dixon

Ginger Miller

Amirah Hunter

Okneeka Roberts

About the Author

Nichole Harmon-Pointdujour is a Wall Street executive and the CEO of The Master Connector Agency, with over 20 years of experience in finance, trading, investment banking, operations, program management, business management, diversity, recruiting, philanthropy, and community development.

After beginning her career at one of the top banks In trade support for equities, bonds and options on the trading floor while pursuing her MBA, Nichole joined a prestigious global financial institution's Investment Banking Analyst Program, where she worked on emerging market debt deals. Her career in finance has since spanned roles in treasury middle office, private bank managed accounts equity trading, asset management finance, and executive leadership in community development and national partnerships.

In her executive role, Nichole has managed multi-million dollar budgets, overseen strategic partnerships and civic engagement, as well as grants and sponsorships. She has led significant initiatives including a program that has donated more than 1,050 mortgage-free homes to veterans and military families with over $200 million in investments. Her leadership in diversity and inclusion initiatives has helped drive efforts to recruit, hire, retain, and advance Black talent across multiple organizations.

As founder and CEO of The Master Connector Agency, Nichole hosts exclusive in-person events that bring together top corporate executives from Fortune 500 companies, government officials, and industry leaders. These carefully curated gatherings—called "The Rooms Where the Deals Are Done"—feature celebrity keynote speakers and are limited to just 150 select individuals to ensure meaningful networking opportunities that enhance both connections and net worth.

An avid international traveler who has visited over 40 countries, Nichole is a staunch supporter of all branches of the United States military and underrepresented communities. She volunteers as a mentor with Children's Aid, a non-profit that exposes students from Harlem and the Bronx to financial institutions. She is the proud recipient of the Women's in Service Award from the Women's Veterans Interactive Organization.

Nichole holds a bachelor's degree from Virginia Union University and a master's in business management from Strayer University.

ABOUT THE AUTHOR

To learn more about Nichole's work and to join The Master Connector membership community, where you can receive monthly coaching directly from Nichole and connect with like-minded professionals dedicated to building powerful relationships, visit www.TheMasterConnectorAgency.com.

Sign up for the exclusive Connectors Community membership to access strategic networking resources, attend virtual coaching sessions, and be the first to learn about upcoming events where deals are made and opportunities are created.

Praise for The Master Connector

"Brilliant! Nichole is a natural connector who has quite literally mastered the art of networking to build meaningful relationships. Her introductions have been pivotal in helping me and others move the needle in our businesses. I am happy she is finally able to share her gift with the masses."
- *Egypt Sherrod,* **TV Personality, Speaker, CEO of Indigo Road Realty & Design**

"There are many people who are born with exceptional talent. Beyoncé has mastered the art of singing and performing, Beethoven was a master composer and pianist, and now there is Nichole Harmon - Pointdujour; she is the Master Connector. She has revolutionized the art of networking. Her emotionally sound discernment of putting the right people in rooms has led to intense bonds and wide-ranging connections bridging gaps of success in every arena, from corporate to sports and entertainment."
- *Yandy Smith Harris,* **TV Personality, Speaker, Entrepreneur & Media Mogul**

"Empowered women EMPOWER women. As The Master Connector, Nichole believes in the strength of sisterhood. She believes that together we can elevate dreams, build legacies, and create a thriving community of black female entrepreneurs by uplifting and supporting each other. Thank you for bringing together a network of talented women and helping transform our female community, one connection at a time."
- ***Cynthia Bailey,*** **Actor, TV Personality, Women's Health Advocate**

"The secret ingredient to success is cultivating trust and building relationships that are not transactional. Nichole Harmon - Pointdujour's The Master Connector is a riveting book on navigating complexity, conquering your dreams, and delivering sustained impact. This book is a must-read masterpiece."
- ***Valeisha Butterfield,*** **Award-winning leader**

"Nichole Harmon-Pointdujour is an absolute force when it comes to making connections that matter. As someone who's spent years investing in groundbreaking ideas and visionary leaders, I can tell you that Nichole's unparalleled ability to unite people is nothing short of revolutionary. This book isn't just another read—it's a blueprint for unlocking the kind of relationships that transform lives and spark lifelong success. Nichole's approach is refreshingly genuine and bursting with energy. Her knack for linking the right people at the right time reminds me of what my dear friend always emphasizes: that the real currency in life is the network you build.

PRAISE FOR THE MASTER CONNECTOR

And believe me, Nichole has mastered that art. If you're ready to shift your perspective, fuel your ambitions, and tap into the most dynamic connections imaginable, this book is your next must-read. Get ready to be inspired, empowered, and forever changed!"
- *Ian Dunlap,* **The Master Investor & Founder of Red Panda**

To my dearest oldest daughter, "Nichole," as a blessed, devoted corporate career-driven working woman before and after your MBA, you have always found the strength to face challenges with confidence, being an inspirational light to others while making important relationships and business connections. Witnessing your achievements makes me a proud mother of your many accomplishments, including your amazing adventures and journey while traveling to many countries in the world. May you always keep God first and help others along the way with your awesome business as "The Master Connector." Listen to your heart and be yourself. Always remember how much you are truly loved. Love you always & forever!
- *Valerie* **Harmon-Parker (Mom)**

"Even at a young age, Nichole would attract all types of people, and she treated them the same—with love and compassion. It didn't matter if they were homeless or a CEO of a Fortune 500 company. So, it was a natural progression that she would become the Master Connector."
- *Brian Parker* **(Dad)**

"Your authenticity and warmth are truly magnetic. The connections you cultivate are built on love, trust, and

putting God first, and it's evident in everything you do."
- ***Lydell & Brittany Dewberry*** (**Brother & Sister-in-Law**)

"My sister is the embodiment of resilience and confidence. She always moves with sheer determination, proving that no challenge is too great when you decide to own your potential. Fearless, fun, and endlessly energetic, she walks into every room knowing her worth and connects effortlessly with people at all levels. Now, doing what she loves—bringing others together and helping them grow—she inspires everyone around her with her passion, brilliance, and unshakable belief in herself."
- ***Brianna Parker*** (**Sister**)

"Nichole's ability to connect people from all walks of life is remarkable. Her radiant presence lights up any room, and her success in building her agency and Connectors Community speaks for itself. This book shares the secrets to her success as a Master Connector."
- ***Greg Pointdujour*** (**Husband**)

"From her humble beginnings, Nichole has always recognized the immense power of authentic relationships to elevate and empower those around her. Over the years, she has tirelessly bridged the gap between driven individuals—often overlooked or unsure how to communicate their value—and the corporate leaders who can provide the partnerships and opportunities they need to thrive. Nichole's unwavering commitment to connecting people reflects her belief that true success is born from

the bonds we form and the doors we open for one another."
- *Zackary Simmons-Glover* (**Brother**)

"I have known Nichole since we were in high school, and since then, she has always led with positive energy that is infectious. Her tenacity to make connections, her unwillingness to accept "no" when she believes "yes" is the only option, and her unwavering passion for engagement in this business world are collectively just a small part of what sets her apart from others. All the while, she has never forgotten where she came from. Nichole deserves all accolades bestowed onto her and the continued successes that frankly are inevitable given her earnestness to win, not simply for herself but for her community at large."
- *Arinze Onugha,* **ESQ**

"Nichole's passion for people is evident through every connection she creates. She has mastered the skill of building meaningful and impactful relationships that bring together individuals from different backgrounds and perspectives to create a cohesive force. She fosters spaces for collaboration, sparks innovation, and she knows someone in every business sector! Nichole's magnetic energy enables her to enter high-class, elite rooms, yet it doesn't change who she is at her core—humble, caring, selfless, and an overall amazing individual. I'm proud to call her my friend and am excited that she is sharing her story, tools, and tips on how to embrace the power of human interaction."
- *Tiffany Cobb*

"Nichole is a force of nature—an incredible person with a heart for impact and an unmatched ability to bring the right people together. Her powerful connections don't just open doors; they create opportunities that transform lives. The Master Connector Agency isn't just a brand—it's a movement that's going to change the world by bridging the gap between visionaries and the resources they need to thrive."
- ***Ebony Frazier***

"After connecting with Nichole, I have had the opportunity to be in the room with top-tier celebrities, A+ entertainers, entrepreneurs, politicians, CEOs, etc. Nichole strives and motivates her team members to pursue their goals; she offers positive feedback, and she always leads by example. I appreciate you, Nichole (The Master Connector), and your connections and look forward to the future."
- ***Pamela Tucker***

"The true power of networking lies in bridging worlds—bringing together people from all walks of life to create opportunities, spark ideas, and build something greater than themselves. Nichole truly embodies this; she has a rare gift not just for meeting people but genuinely connecting them. She doesn't just open doors; she builds pathways to life-changing opportunities."
- ***Shannon Carter***

"I'm beyond proud of my lifelong friend, Nichole. We've been through so much together, and I've watched her grow

into the ultimate connector. Whether it's across states or even continents, she's always been that social butterfly, effortlessly building relationships and sharing her network to help others succeed—all while balancing school, working in finance, and traveling the world. She's truly found her calling!"
- ***Corlette Dixon***

"Nichole is more than just a Master Connector—she is a dynamic Change Agent for good, a force to be reckoned with. I have been truly blessed by her unwavering determination and her extraordinary ability to connect the right people for the greatest impact. With an innate gift for fostering meaningful connections and the tenacity to turn vision into action, Nichole is a powerhouse of purpose and transformation."
- ***Ginger Miller*, President & CEO, Women Veterans Interactive Foundation**

"Nichole has always been exceptional at bringing people together. She is now using that gift to launch her brand and connect individuals through a broad network. Truly the master connector!"
- ***Amirah Hunter***

"For over 15 years, Nichole has been a thoughtful, consistent, and family-oriented sister friend—one of the most multifaceted women I've ever had the pleasure of knowing. Her gift for connecting people is more than just a skill; it's a calling that she has embraced with authenticity, kindness, and purpose. Watching her not only change lives through these connections but also rightfully monetize her impact is both inspiring and well-deserved. Congrats, Nich!"

- *O'Kneeka Roberts,* **Sales Strategist OI Roberts Consultancy**

www.ingramcontent.com/pod-product-compliance
Lightning Source LLC
Chambersburg PA
CBHW070128080526
44586CB00015B/1602